EXPRESS MEDITERRANEAN DIET INSTANT POT COOKBOOK

Wholesome, Easy, Mouth-Watering and Healthy Mediterranean Instant Pot Recipes for Beginners

Jennifer Champlin

© Copyright 2020 - All rights reserved.

The content contained within this book may not be reproduced, duplicated or transmitted without direct written permission from the author or the publisher.

Under no circumstances will any blame or legal responsibility be held against the publisher, or author, for any damages, reparation, or monetary loss due to the information contained within this book, either directly or indirectly.

Legal Notice:

This book is copyright protected. It is only for personal use. You cannot amend, distribute, sell, use, quote or paraphrase any part, or the content within this book, without the consent of the author or publisher.

Disclaimer Notice:

Please note the information contained within this document is for educational and entertainment purposes only. All effort has been executed to present accurate, up to date, reliable, complete information. No warranties of any kind are declared or implied. Readers acknowledge that the author is not engaged in the rendering of legal, financial, medical or professional advice. The content within this book has been derived from various sources. Please consult a licensed professional before attempting any techniques outlined in this book.

By reading this document, the reader agrees that under no circumstances is the author responsible for any losses, direct or indirect, that are incurred as a result of the use of the information contained within this document, including, but not limited to, errors, omissions, or inaccuracies.

Table of Contents

Introduction 1

Chapter 1: About the Mediterranean Diet 3

    Benefits of the Mediterranean Diet 4

        Lower Risk of Cardiovascular Diseases 4

        Increased Agility 5

        Reduced Risk of Alzheimer's Disease 5

        Weight Loss and Maintenance 6

        Increased Longevity 6

        Lower Risk of Parkinson's Disease 6

        Reduced Risk and Better Management of Type 2 Diabetes 7

Chapter 2: Electric Pot Mediterranean Diet Breakfast Recipes 9

    Mediterranean Egg Bites 9

    Berry Cobbler Oats 12

    Coconut Cranberry Quinoa 14

    Mediterranean Mini Frittatas 16

    Mediterranean Breakfast Casserole 18

    Superfood Instant Pot Oatmeal Jars 20

Multigrain Breakfast Bowl 22

Spinach Frittata 25

Greek Yogurt 27

Traditional Instant Pot Oatmeal 30

Instant Pot Scallion Omelet 32

Chapter 3: Electric Pot Mediterranean Diet Snack and Dip Recipes 34

Greek Salad Egg Bites 34

Shrimp Appetizers with Avocado and Cucumber 36

Mediterranean Deviled Eggs 38

Steamed Artichokes with Mediterranean Aioli 40

Corn on the Cob 43

Chipotle Pomegranate Taco Bites 45

Butter Corn Kernels 47

Garlic and Butter Mushrooms 49

3-2-1 Dip 51

Mediterranean Pizza Dip 53

White Kidney Beans/Cannellini Beans Dip 55

Hummus 57

Chapter 4: Mediterranean Diet Soup, Chili, and Stew Recipes 59

Classic Minestrone Soup 59

Chicken and Cauliflower Rice Soup 62

Vegan Cabbage Detox Soup 65

Red Lentil and Yellow Split Pea Soup 67

Chicken Posole Verde 69

Chicken Chili with White Beans 71

Turkey Chili 73

Italian Beef Stew with Sage and Red Wine 75

Middle Eastern Lamb Stew 77

Brazilian Fish Stew 80

Mediterranean Chicken and Quinoa Stew 83

African Chicken and Peanut Stew 85

Chapter 5: Mediterranean Diet Salad Recipes 88

Salad Nicoise 88

Crunchy Noodle Salad 91

Warm White Bean Salad 94

Tuna Pasta Salad 96

Avocado Egg Salad 98

Instant Pot Beet Salad with Yogurt, Lime & Jalapeño 100

Chicken Bacon Avocado Salad 102

Chapter 6: Mediterranean Diet Lunch Recipes 105

Mediterranean Spinach-Feta Pie 105

Greek Chicken Tacos 108

Ground Turkey Quinoa Bowls 111

Black Eyed Peas with Fresh Dill and Parsley 113

Acorn Squash Stuffed with Cranberries, Wild Rice, and Chickpeas 115

Spanish Chicken and Rice 118

Italian Chicken and Broccoli Bowls 120

Turkey Bolognese 122

Chapter 7: Mediterranean Diet Poultry Recipes 125

Spicy Chicken Shawarma 125

Tuscan Chicken 128

Caprese Chicken Thighs 130

Chicken Cacciatore 132

Jambalaya 134

Spicy Mediterranean Chicken 137

Turkey Meatballs and Spaghetti Squash 139

Enchilada Pasta 142

Chapter 8: Mediterranean Diet Meat Recipes 144

Sloppy Joes 144

Beef Stuffed Peppers 147

Shepherd's Pie with Potatoes and Yams 149

Beef Fajitas 153

Mediterranean Instant Pot Shredded Beef 156

Mediterranean Pork Tenderloin with Couscous 158

Green Beans with Pork and Potatoes 161

Mediterranean Leg of Lamb Roast.. 163

Mediterranean Lamb Shanks 166

Chapter 9: Mediterranean Seafood Recipes 169

Instant Pot Frozen Salmon.. 169

Salmon Fillets and Vegetables..171

Mediterranean Pasta with Tuna and Tomatoes................... 173

Italian Fish 175

Lemon Pepper Salmon 177

Paella with Cauliflower Rice 180

Shrimp Fra Diavolo Pasta 183

Salmon with Chili Lime Sauce 185

Quick and Easy Shrimp Curry 187

One Pot Shrimp and Veggies 189

Shrimp and Tomatoes with Warm Spices............................... 191

Tomato and Shrimp Orzo...194

Chapter 10: Mediterranean Diet Vegetarian Recipes 196

Makhani Daal (Buttery Lentils)... 196

Two Bean Burritos 199

Farro with Tomatoes 201

Barley Risotto with Tomatoes and Marinated Feta........... 203

Vegetable Lasagna 206

Spring Vegetable Brown Rice Risotto 209

Whole Wheat Spaghetti with Marinara 211

Moroccan Baked Beans 212

Chapter 11: Mediterranean Diet Vegan Recipes 214

Chickpeas with Salsa Verde 214

BBQ Lentil Sloppy Joes 217

Portobello Pot Roast 220

Fasolakia (Green Beans and Potatoes in Olive Oil) 223

Lentil Curry 225

Quinoa Burrito Bowls 227

Moroccan Lentils 229

Spinach Mushroom Pasta 231

Lentil Loaf 234

Tofu & Green Beans Curry 237

Chapter 12: Mediterranean Diet Side Dish Recipes 240

Ratatouille 240

Black Rice Risotto with Mushrooms and Caramelized
Onions 243

Instant Pot Twice Baked Potatoes 246

Mediterranean Vegetables 249

Mediterranean Rice 251

Instant Pot Artichokes 253

Horta (Greens) and Potatoes.. 255

Instant Pot Cabbage 257

Scalloped Potatoes.. 259

Instant Pot Roasted Brussels Sprouts..................................... 261

Chapter 13: Mediterranean Diet Dessert Recipes 263

Mediterranean Diet Friendly Cake... 263

Apple Crisp 266

French Lemon Crème (Pots de Crème au Citron)............ 268

Rice Pudding with Cranberries 270

Bread Pudding... 272

Mixed Berry Crumble 274

Crème Brulee 276

Poached Pears 278

Pumpkin Custard..280

Conclusion 282

References 284

INTRODUCTION

I want to thank you for choosing this book Mediterranean Electric Pot Cookbook - Wholesome, Easy, and Mouth-Watering Electric Pot Recipes for Beginners. I hope you find it useful in preparing wholesome, easy, and mouth-watering meals using your electric pot.

Our modern-day diet is filled with "on the run food," and more often than not, most of us end up eating a lot of unhealthy food in the bargain. Our diet is one of the major factors that lead to some of the most common health conditions such as obesity, type 2 diabetes, and cardiovascular diseases. Food plays a crucial role in maintaining the health of our body, its optimal functions, and its longevity. One of the best ways to ensure good health is by eating healthy food, and that is exactly what this cookbook will help you do.

The first step to bring about a change in your health is to watch what you eat. Instead of eating junk food or going out for meals often, you need to start cooking your meals at home and eat a balanced diet. You can go the easy route and choose any random recipe, or you can choose a systematic approach and stick to a dietary pattern that helps you maintain your overall health. Of all the dietary approaches out there, the Mediterranean diet is one of the most widely followed diet plans. There are numerous studies that have demonstrated that the Mediterranean way of eating is extremely beneficial for your health.

This book is a treasure trove of sorts for those who want to learn Mediterranean cooking in an electric pot. We know that you don't have the time or energy to toil over the stove for hours every day. This is why we set out to develop recipes that can be prepared with minimal fuss by using the instant pot. It has a very hands-off approach to cooking since this small device does most of the work for you.

The recipes in this cookbook and the Instant Pot will help you prepare some great meals every single day without a lot of work and without wasting money on takeout. It will also help you to efficiently go about meal prepping so you don't have to worry about what you need to cook every day. If you want to get started with eating your way to good health, start cooking with our cookbook!

Thank you once again for choosing this book. Let's read on and learn more.

CHAPTER 1:
ABOUT THE MEDITERRANEAN DIET

The Mediterranean diet cannot be defined with just a few particulars. It is a culmination of the eating habits of the various regions around the Mediterranean Sea. You may think that the Mediterranean diet is all about lamb chops, pizza, or pasta but it really isn't. These popular dishes are not really a part of their regular diet at all. The real Mediterranean diet is a blend of many healthy foods that have allowed the Mediterranean people to have a higher than average life expectancy and lower risk of diseases. This is why the diet of this region has gained a lot of popularity all over the world in recent years. People are trying to adopt this diet in order to improve their own eating habits and reap the benefits.

So what is the Mediterranean diet? This diet emphasizes the importance of consuming higher amounts of fresh fruits, vegetables, legumes, nuts, whole grains, and seafood and controlled amounts of meat or poultry. Following this diet has proven to be extremely beneficial for the people of that region as well as others who have adopted it. The diet is not just about the food either, as it stresses the importance of regular physical activity for physical health. It also encourages the habit of sharing meals with others as a way to improve your mental well-being.

However, it is not easy to make a sudden drastic change to your diet. Especially when you consume a lot of processed foods and eat out a lot. But if you are willing and try to switch to this Mediterranean diet, you will reap its benefits and see a significant improvement in your health. This diet is a fairly inexpensive way of eating, and the electric pot ensures that you don't have to put in too much work when preparing your meals either.

Benefits of the Mediterranean Diet

There are several health benefits of the Mediterranean diet that are backed up by a lot of studies. Here is a look at some of the common health benefits of the diet based on the latest research (Martini D., 2019).

Lower Risk of Cardiovascular Diseases

An unhealthy diet is a major precursor for the development of heart disease. However, the Mediterranean diet will help you limit your intake of any refined or processed foods that affect your health. This diet also encourages a single glass of red wine instead of drinking any hard liquor. Red wine has proven benefits for heart health if consumed in a controlled manner.

Increased Agility

This diet is also especially beneficial for older adults as it allows them to consume a lot of nutrients that prevent muscle weakness. It reduces the person's tendency to become frail over the years as well. It allows an older person on the Mediterranean diet to remain more agile than other elderly people who follow a different diet.

Reduced Risk of Alzheimer's Disease

According to research, this diet can also help improve cholesterol levels (Scarmeas N. *et al.*, 2006). While an average Western diet increases bad LDL cholesterol levels, this diet increases good HDL cholesterol levels instead. It reduces the consumption of sugar as well. Since this diet improves blood vessel health, it reduces the risk of developing Alzheimer's disease.

Weight Loss and Maintenance

People living in Mediterranean regions are a lot less prone to develop weight-related issues. Their healthy diet and lifestyle habits ensure that they can remain healthy while avoiding excessive weight gain. This diet can also help you lose weight and maintain the weight loss in the long term.

Increased Longevity

A lot of the world's centenarians live in the Mediterranean region. Their diet plays a major role in contributing to their longevity. The food they consume reduces the risk of diseases like cancer and cardiovascular issues, which helps to increase life expectancy.

Lower Risk of Parkinson's Disease

The Mediterranean diet contains foods with high amounts of antioxidants. These antioxidants help fight oxidative stress in the body. Since oxidative stress is a damaging process that increases the risk of Parkinson's disease, following the Mediterranean diet naturally lowers the risk of developing Parkinson's disease.

Reduced Risk and Better Management of Type 2 Diabetes

This diet is rich in fiber and aids in slower digestion. This slower digestion, in turn, keeps you feeling full for a longer time and thus prevents random hunger cravings. It also prevents blood sugar levels from fluctuating. The Mediterranean diet helps in losing weight and also protects again the development of type 2 diabetes.

Unlike what a lot of people assume, it does not cost a lot of money to follow this diet. You just have to consume more wholesome and fresh foods as opposed to processed and refined foods. Your main source of protein will be lentils and beans. Instead of refined grains, you will consume more whole grains that are better for your body. Making a whole Mediterranean meal will be much more cost-effective than going out to eat or buying processed goods.

You also have to remember to keep your red wine consumption to a moderate level. It is only beneficial for your body if consumed in limited amounts. Too much of it will affect your heart in a negative way.

The Mediterranean diet is not about consuming a lot of cheesy pasta and bread. Those who live in the Mediterranean generally consume pasta like a side dish, in small portions, unlike the way Americans eat it. Most of the plate is filled with vegetables, salads, fish, and some grass-fed meat if any. They don't have more than a slice or two of bread if it is included in the meal.

Don't overlook the other lifestyle habits that the people in this region follow if you want to reap the benefits of the diet. It is not just about the food. Use the recipes given here to prepare wholesome meals but also try to become more active. This will help you resolve most of your weight and health issues. The recipes will be divided into courses and meals so you can easily plan and prep your meals in advance.

PS: I use an Instant Pot for my cooking, but you are free to use any multicooker of your choice.

CHAPTER 2:
ELECTRIC POT MEDITERRANEAN DIET BREAKFAST RECIPES

MEDITERRANEAN EGG BITES

Preparation time: 10 minutes

Cooking time: 15 – 18 minutes

Number of servings: 6 (2 bites each)

Ingredients:

- 2 tablespoons olive oil
- 1 cup diced sweet red pepper
- 1 cup diced onion
- Salt to taste
- 12 eggs
- ½ cup milk of your choice
- ¾ cup chopped feta cheese
- Salt to taste

- 8 tablespoons chopped sun-dried tomatoes
- 4 tablespoon chopped parsley
- Pepper to taste

Directions:

1. Select the 'Sauté' button. Add oil and allow it to heat. Add red pepper, onion, and salt and cook until the onions turn translucent, stirring occasionally. Select the 'Cancel' button.
2. Remove the onion mixture and place in a bowl. Wipe the pot clean.
3. Pour a cup of water into your electric pot.
4. Add eggs, milk, salt, and pepper into a bowl and whisk it well.
5. Stir in the rest of the ingredients. Also add the sautéed onion mixture and stir.
6. Grease an egg bite mold with cooking spray.
7. Place a trivet in the electric pot. Place the egg bite mold on the trivet. Divide the egg mixture into 12 egg bite cavities in the mold.
8. Keep the mold covered loosely with foil.

9. Close the lid and lock it by setting the valve to the sealed position. Select the 'Manual' button. Set the timer for 8 minutes.

10. When the timer goes off, allow the pressure to release naturally for 5 minutes, after which quickly release the excess pressure.

11. Remove the mold from the pot and set aside to cool for a few minutes on your countertop.

12. If necessary, run a knife around the edges of the egg bites to loosen them.

13. Invert onto a plate. Serve warm as it is or with toasted and buttered bread if desired.

BERRY COBBLER OATS

Preparation time: 5 minutes

Cooking time: 15 minutes

Number of servings: 4

Ingredients:

- ½ tablespoon coconut oil
- 1 ½ cups water
- ½ cup steel cut oats
- 1 ½ tablespoons maple syrup
- ½ cup dark cherries, pitted
- ½ cup blueberries
- ½ teaspoon salt
- ½ tablespoon fresh lemon juice
- ¼ cup chopped walnuts

Directions:

1. Select the 'Sauté' button. Add oil and allow it to heat. Add oats and stir fry until golden brown. Select the 'Cancel' button.

2. Stir in salt and pour in the water.

3. Close the lid and lock it by setting the valve to the seal position. Select the 'Manual' button. Set the timer for 10 minutes.

4. When the timer goes off, allow the pressure to release naturally for 5 minutes, after which quickly release the excess pressure.

5. Add maple syrup, walnuts, berries, and lemon juice and stir.

6. Divide into 4 bowls and serve.

COCONUT CRANBERRY QUINOA

Preparation time: 5 minutes

Cooking time: 10 minutes

Number of servings: 2

Ingredients:

- ½ cup quinoa, rinsed
- 1 ½ cups coconut water
- 1 tablespoon pure maple syrup or agave nectar
- 2 tablespoons dried cranberries
- 1 tablespoon almonds, sliced
- 1 tablespoon coconut flakes

Directions:

1. Combine all the ingredients in the instant pot.
2. Close the lid and lock it by setting the valve to the sealed position. Select the 'Manual' button. Set the timer for 1 minute.

3. When the timer goes off, allow the pressure to release naturally for about 8 minutes, after which quickly release the excess pressure.
4. Fluff with a fork and serve.

MEDITERRANEAN MINI FRITTATAS

Preparation time: 10 minutes

Cooking time: 5 minutes

Number of servings: 6 (2 mini frittatas each)

Ingredients:

- 3 large eggs
- Salt to taste
- 3 tablespoons pitted kalamata olives, drained, chopped
- Freshly ground pepper to taste
- ¼ cup sun-dried tomatoes in oil, drained, chopped
- 2 tablespoons crumbled feta
- 2 tablespoons bottled sweet red peppers, drained, chopped
- 2 tablespoons shredded Asiago cheese
- 2 tablespoons chopped flat-leaf parsley
- 2 tablespoons half and half or milk
- 2 tablespoons thinly sliced artichokes in oil, drained

Directions:

1. Pour a cup of water into the instant pot.
2. Add eggs, salt, pepper, and half and half or milk into the blender and blend until smooth.
3. Grease an egg bite mold with some cooking spray.
4. Place a trivet in the instant pot. Place the egg bite mold on the trivet. Divide the egg mixture into 12 egg bite cavities in the mold.
5. Divide the remaining ingredients equally among the cavities and stir lightly.
6. Keep the mold covered loosely with foil.
7. Close the lid and lock it by setting the valve to the sealed position. Select the 'Manual' button. Set the timer for 8 minutes.
8. When the timer goes off, allow the pressure to release naturally for 5 minutes, after which quickly release the excess pressure.
9. Remove the mold from the pot and set aside to cool completely on your countertop.
10. If necessary, run a knife around the edges of the egg bites to loosen them.
11. Invert onto a plate and serve.

MEDITERRANEAN BREAKFAST CASSEROLE

Preparation time: 10 minutes

Cooking time: 15 minutes

Number of servings: 4

Ingredients:

- 2 tablespoons plain almond milk, unsweetened
- 1 tablespoon chopped fresh oregano leaves
- 1/8 teaspoon freshly ground black pepper
- 6 tablespoons feta cheese, crumbled
- ¼ cup sliced green onions
- 2 canned artichoke hearts in water, chopped
- 1/3 cup sliced mushrooms
- 2 large egg whites
- 4 large eggs
- 1 tablespoon low-fat parmesan cheese, grated
- ½ teaspoon garlic powder
- 2 cloves garlic, sliced
- ½ teaspoon paprika

- 2 ounces baby spinach
- ½ teaspoon sea salt or to taste

Directions:

1. Add eggs, whites, oregano, garlic powder, milk, salt, and pepper to a large bowl. Whisk until well combined. Add parmesan and feta cheese and whisk it well.
2. Grease the instant pot insert pan (or any heatproof pan that can fit well inside the instant pot) with some oil.
3. Layer the spinach, tomatoes, artichoke, garlic, green onion, and mushrooms in the dish.
4. Pour the egg mixture into the dish. Fold lightly.
5. Pour a cup of water into the instant pot.
6. Place a trivet in the instant pot. Place the baking dish on the trivet.
7. Close the lid and lock it by setting the valve to the sealed position. Select the 'Manual' button. Set the timer for 15 minutes.
8. When the timer goes off, allow the pressure to release naturally.
9. Let it cool for 10 minutes.
10. Slice into wedges and serve.

SUPERFOOD INSTANT POT OATMEAL JARS

Preparation time: 5 minutes

Cooking time: 9 minutes

Number of servings: 3

Ingredients:

For oatmeal:

- ¾ cup rolled oats
- ½ apple, cored, chopped
- 3 tablespoons raisins or goji berries
- 2 – 3 tablespoons chia seeds or flaxseeds
- A pinch sea salt
- 2 cups almond milk
- 1 medium carrot, cut into matchsticks
- 1/3 cup chopped walnuts
- 1 teaspoon ground cinnamon
- 2 tablespoons maple syrup or coconut sugar (optional)

To serve:

- Almond milk
- Fresh blueberries
- ¼ cup light cream or non-dairy cream
- Any other fresh fruit of your choice
- 1 – 2 teaspoons protein powder (optional)

Directions:

1. Spray the inside of the cooking pot with some cooking spray.
2. Add all the ingredients for the oatmeal into the instant pot and stir.
3. Close the lid and lock it by setting the valve to the sealed position. Select the 'Manual' button. Set the timer for 8 – 9 minutes.
4. When the timer goes off, allow the pressure to release naturally for 3 minutes, after which quickly release the excess pressure.
5. Open the lid and let it rest for 3 minutes. Stir in protein powder and cream.
6. Divide into 4 Mason's jars (8 ounces each).
7. Serve with almond milk, blueberries, and any fresh fruit.

MULTIGRAIN BREAKFAST BOWL

Preparation time: 10 minutes

Cooking time: 10 minutes

Number of servings: 4

Ingredients:

- ½ cup steel-cut oats
- ¼ cup dry millet
- ½ cup dry golden quinoa
- 1 ½ tablespoons olive oil, divided
- Juice of a large lemon
- Zest of 1 lemon, grated
- ½ inch fresh ginger, thinly sliced
- ¼ cup maple syrup
- 1/8 teaspoon ground nutmeg
- ¼ cup chopped strawberries
- ¼ cup blueberries
- ¼ cup raspberries
- ¼ cup blackberries

- ½ cup Greek yogurt or soy yogurt
- 1 cup chopped hazelnuts, toasted
- 2 ¼ cups water
- ¼ teaspoon + 1/8 teaspoon salt

Directions:

1. Place all the grains in a fine wire mesh strainer and rinse under running tap water. Keep the strainer over a bowl for about 5 minutes.

2. Select the 'Sauté' button. Add ½ tablespoon of oil. Once the oil is hot enough, add the oats, millet, and quinoa and stir fry for a few minutes until toasted and aromatic. Press the 'Cancel' button.

3. Add salt, half the lemon zest, and ginger slices and stir.

4. Close the lid and lock it by setting the valve to the sealed position. Select the 'Manual' button. Set the timer for 1 minute.

5. When the timer goes off, allow the pressure to release naturally for about 8 minutes, after which quickly release the excess pressure. Do not open the lid for a couple of minutes.

6. Open the lid and loosen the grains with a fork. Discard the ginger slices.

7. Transfer onto a baking sheet and set aside to cool.

8. Add the grains and remaining lemon zest into a bowl. Toss well.

9. Add all the berries and toss well.

10. Add lemon juice and 1 tablespoon oil into a bowl and whisk until the mixture emulsifies.

11. Add maple syrup, nutmeg, and yogurt and whisk it well. Drizzle over the grains and toss well.

12. Add hazelnuts and toss well. Cover and chill for 7 – 8 hours.

13. Serve.

SPINACH FRITTATA

Preparation time: 5 minutes

Cooking time: 15 minutes

Number of servings: 3

Ingredients:

- 3 eggs
- ½ teaspoon dried oregano
- ¼ teaspoon pepper or to taste
- ¼ cup diced, deseeded fresh tomatoes
- 2 tablespoons chopped Spanish olives
- ¼ cup frozen spinach, thawed, drained of excess moisture
- 2 tablespoons milk
- Salt to taste
- 2 tablespoons chopped kalamata olives
- 2 tablespoon crumbled feta cheese

Directions:

1. Spray some cooking spray in the instant pot insert pan or any other heatproof pan that can fit well inside the instant pot.

2. Add eggs, garlic powder, milk, salt, oregano, and garlic powder into a bowl and whisk it well.

3. Add the remaining ingredients and stir. Transfer into the insert pan.

4. Place a steaming rack or trivet in the instant pot. Pour 1 cup water into it. Place the dish on the rack.

5. Close the lid and lock it by setting the valve to the sealed position. Select the 'Manual' button. Set the timer for 15 minutes.

6. When the timer goes off, allow the pressure to release naturally for 7 – 8 minutes, after which quickly release the excess pressure.

7. Open the lid and let it rest for 3 – 4 minutes.

8. Cut into wedges and serve.

GREEK YOGURT

Preparation time: 5 minutes

Cooking time: 35 minutes + resting time of about 8 hours

Number of servings: 5 - 8

Ingredients:

For whole milk yogurt:

- 1 tablespoon yogurt starter
- 8 cups whole milk fat-free

For low-fat yogurt:

- 1 tablespoon yogurt starter
- 8 cups 1% or 2% milk

To serve: Use any (optional)

- Berries of your choice
- Fresh fruit of your choice
- Granola
- Chopped dried fruit and nuts

Directions:

1. To sterilize the cooking pot (this is optional): Pour 3 cups of water into the instant pot.

2. Close the lid and lock it by setting the valve to the sealed position. Select the 'Steam' button and set the timer for 5 minutes.

3. When the timer goes off, quickly release the excess pressure and discard the water. Wipe the pot with a clean kitchen towel until dry.

4. For whole milk yogurt: Add milk into the pot. If you have the glass lid (accessory), use it. Otherwise, use the instant pot lid.

5. Close the lid. Select the 'Yogurt' button and press the 'Adjust' button until it displays 'Boil'. Whisk the milk a few times until it displays 'Boil'. Cover the pot after whisking each time. Press the 'Cancel' button.

6. When it displays 'Boil', uncover and let the milk cool to between 95°F and 110°F.

7. Take out 4 – 5 tablespoons of the warm milk and add into a bowl. Add the yogurt starter and whisk it well. Add this mixture into the pot and whisk it well. Close the lid.

8. Select the 'Yogurt' button. The preset time should typically be 8 hours. Otherwise, adjust it to 8 hours as

this is how long it will take to set. Do not disturb the mixture during this time.

9. Take out the cooking pot. Cool for a few hours in the refrigerator. Do not disturb the pot once again during this time.

10. For low-fat yogurt: All the steps remain the same as in whole milk yogurt. However, the yogurt should be allowed to set for 14 hours instead of 8 hours.

11. To make Greek yogurt: Place a yogurt strainer on a bowl. Add the yogurt into the strainer.

12. Place the bowl along with the strainer in the refrigerator for about 2 hours. The strained liquid is whey and should be whitish in color. If you don't have a yogurt strainer, then place a piece of cheesecloth in a strainer and strain the yogurt.

13. The yogurt that is remaining in the strainer is Greek yogurt.

14. Serve your Greek yogurt with any of the suggested serving options.

15. For vanilla-flavored yogurt, add a teaspoon of vanilla extract when you pour milk into the pot.

TRADITIONAL INSTANT POT OATMEAL

Preparation time: 5 minutes

Cooking time: 25 minutes

Number of servings: 2

Ingredients:

- 1 ¼ - 1 ½ cups water
- ½ cup steel cut oats or old-fashioned oats

Serving options: Use any

- Almond milk
- Fresh berries of your choice
- Fresh fruit of your choice
- Nut butter
- Dried fruit or nuts
- Date paste
- Coconut flakes
- Flaxseeds or chia seeds, etc.

Directions:

1. Place oats in the cooking pot of the instant pot. Pour water over them.

2. Close the lid and lock it by setting the valve to the sealed position. Select the 'Porridge' button. Set the timer for 15 minutes.

3. When the timer goes off, quickly release the excess pressure.

4. Open the lid and let it rest for 3 – 4 minutes before serving.

INSTANT POT SCALLION OMELET

Preparation time: 5 minutes

Cooking time: 20 minutes

Number of servings: 4

Ingredients:

- 6 eggs
- ¼ teaspoon garlic powder
- Freshly ground pepper to taste
- ¼ teaspoon sesame seeds
- Salt to taste
- 5 – 6 tablespoons water
- ¼ teaspoon red pepper flakes
- 4 scallions, chopped

Directions:

1. Pour a cup of water into the cooking pot in the instant pot. Place a trivet in it.
2. Whisk together eggs, water, salt, and spices in a bowl.

3. Divide the mixture into a ramekin and place it over the trivet.

4. Close the lid and lock it by setting the valve to the sealed position. Select the 'Manual' button. Set the timer for 5 minutes.

5. When the timer goes off, allow the pressure to release naturally for 10 minutes and then quickly release the excess pressure.

6. Open the lid and let it rest for 3 – 4 minutes.

7. Serve.

CHAPTER 3:
ELECTRIC POT MEDITERRANEAN DIET SNACK AND DIP RECIPES

GREEK SALAD EGG BITES

Preparation time: 15 minutes

Cooking time: 20 minutes

Number of servings: 12 – 14

Ingredients:

- 1 ½ cups (¼ inch cubes) feta
- 1 medium tomato, deseeded, finely chopped, discard all the liquid from the tomato
- 1 cup ricotta cheese
- ½ teaspoon paprika
- 1 teaspoon finely chopped fresh oregano leaves
- ½ teaspoon dried oregano
- 20 Greek olives, pitted, finely chopped
- 8 large eggs

- ½ teaspoon pepper or to taste
- Salt to taste
- ½ teaspoon paprika or to taste

Directions:

1. Add eggs into a bowl and whisk well. Add ricotta, salt, pepper, dried oregano, and paprika and whisk well.
2. Whisk in the fresh oregano.
3. Stir in feta, tomato, and olives.
4. Grease an egg bite mold with cooking spray.
5. Place a trivet in the instant pot. Place the egg bite mold on the trivet. Divide the egg mixture into 12 – 14 egg bite molds.
6. Keep the mold covered loosely with foil.
7. Close the lid and lock it by setting the valve to the sealed position. Select the 'Manual' button. Set the timer for 10 minutes.
8. When the timer goes off, allow the pressure to release naturally for 10 minutes and then quickly release the excess pressure.
9. Remove the mold from the pot and set aside to cool for a few minutes on your countertop.
10. Loosen the egg bites by running a knife around the edges of the bites. Serve warm or at room temperature.

SHRIMP APPETIZERS WITH AVOCADO AND CUCUMBER

Preparation time: 15 minutes

Cooking time: 4 – 5 minutes

Number of servings: 10 – 12

Ingredients:

For Cajun shrimp:

- ½ pound shrimp, peeled, deveined (10 – 12)
- ½ tablespoon finely chopped cilantro + extra to garnish
- ¼ teaspoon cayenne pepper
- Pepper to taste
- 1 clove garlic, minced
- ½ teaspoon paprika
- ¼ teaspoon sea salt
- 1 tablespoon olive oil, divided

For avocado spread:

- ½ avocado, peeled, pitted, mashed

- ½ tablespoon lime juice + extra to serve
- Salt to taste

To serve:

- ½ English cucumber cut into 10 – 12 round slices

Directions:

1. Dry the shrimp by patting with paper towels.
2. Add shrimp, garlic, paprika, pepper, salt, cayenne pepper, cilantro, and ½ tablespoon olive oil into a bowl and mix well.
3. Select the 'Sauté' button. Add remaining oil. Once the oil is hot enough, spread the shrimp on the bottom of the cooking pot, without overlapping.
4. Cook for 2 minutes undisturbed. Flip and cook the other side for 2 minutes or until it turns pink.
5. To make the avocado spread: Add all the ingredients for avocado spread into a bowl and mix well.
6. To assemble: Place cucumber slices on a large serving platter. Spread avocado spread over the cucumber slices. Place a shrimp on each. Drizzle lime juice on top. Sprinkle cilantro on top and serve.

MEDITERRANEAN DEVILED EGGS

Preparation time: 10 minutes

Cooking time: 5 minutes

Number of servings: 4

Ingredients:

- 4 large eggs
- ¾ teaspoon Dijon mustard or to taste
- ¾ tablespoon coarsely chopped kalamata olives
- ½ tablespoon finely minced parsley
- 1 ½ tablespoons mayonnaise
- ¾ teaspoon white balsamic vinegar
- ¾ tablespoon coarsely chopped capers
- Salt to taste
- Pepper to taste

Directions:

1. Pour 1 cup water into the instant pot. Place a trivet or steamer basket in it.
2. Place the eggs on it.

3. Close the lid and lock it by setting the valve to the sealed position. Select the 'Manual' button. Set the timer for 7 minutes.

4. When the cooking time is over, quickly release the excess pressure.

5. Remove the eggs and place them in a bowl of cold water for a while. Peel the eggs.

6. Separate the yolks from the whites. Place yolks in a bowl and whites on a serving platter.

7. Add the remaining ingredients into the bowl of yolks and stir until the yolks are mashed.

8. Fill the cavities in the whites with the yolk mixture. You can also transfer the yolk mixture into a piping bag and pipe the mixture into the cavities.

9. Serve.

STEAMED ARTICHOKES WITH MEDITERRANEAN AIOLI

Preparation time: 5 minutes

Cooking time: 15 minutes

Number of servings: 6

Ingredients:

For artichokes:

- 2 cups vegetable broth
- 6 medium artichokes, discard stems

For Mediterranean aioli:

- ¼ cup fresh chopped rosemary and oregano
- 1 teaspoon ground coriander
- 2 teaspoons crushed red pepper flakes
- 2 tablespoons mustard or honey mustard
- 1 – 1 1/3 cups olive oil
- 2 tablespoons mayonnaise or Greek yogurt (optional)
- 4 teaspoons minced garlic

- ½ teaspoon ground cumin
- Pepper to taste
- 4 egg yolks
- 4 teaspoons lemon juice
- Salt to taste

Directions:

1. To make the aioli: Blend all the ingredients for aioli in a blender into a smooth paste.
2. Pour the mixture into a bowl. Cover the contents and set it aside in the refrigerator so that the flavors blend together.
3. Place the trivet in the instant pot. Place the artichokes on the trivet, the stem side facing up. Drizzle broth over the artichokes.
4. Close the lid and lock it by setting the valve to the sealed position. Select the 'Steam' button. Set the timer for 15 minutes.
5. When the timer goes off, allow the pressure to release naturally.
6. Take out the artichokes and set aside to cool for a few minutes. When they are cool enough to handle, cut each artichoke into 2 halves.

7. Place the artichoke halves in a large bowl. Pour about ½ cup cooked broth over the artichokes.

8. Serve with aioli.

CORN ON THE COB

Preparation time: 5 minutes

Cooking time: 7 – 10 minutes

Number of servings: 2

Ingredients:

- 2 ears corn, remove the husk
- Spices of your choice
- Salt to taste
- Lemon juice to taste

Directions:

1. Place the steamer basket in the cooking pot. Pour 2 cups of water into the pot. Place corn cobs in the steamer basket.

2. Close the lid and lock it by setting the valve to the sealed position. Select the 'Manual' button. Set the timer for 7 - 10 minutes, depending on the size of the corn.

3. When the timer goes off, allow the pressure to release naturally.

4. Sprinkle salt and spices of your choice. Drizzle lemon juice on the corn and serve.

CHIPOTLE POMEGRANATE TACO BITES

Preparation time: 10 minutes

Cooking time: 20 minutes

Number of servings: 15

Ingredients:

- ½ cup pomegranate juice
- 6 ounces boneless, skinless chicken breast
- ½ teaspoon onion powder
- 1 teaspoon lime juice
- Whole grain tortilla chips to serve
- A handful pomegranate arils
- ½ chipotle pepper in adobo sauce, smashed
- Feta cheese, crumbled, to serve
- ½ teaspoon kosher salt
- ½ teaspoon honey
- ½ tablespoon salsa
- 1 fresh jalapeño, thinly sliced

Directions:

1. Pour pomegranate juice into the cooking pot in the instant pot.

2. Add chicken and chipotle pepper. Sprinkle salt and onion powder.

3. Close the lid and lock it by setting the valve to the sealed position. Select the 'Manual' button. Set the timer for 10 minutes.

4. Allow the pressure to release naturally.

5. Remove the chicken from the pot and transfer it to a cutting board. When it is cool enough to touch, use a pair of forks to shred the chicken.

6. Combine honey, salsa, lime juice, and 3 – 4 tablespoons of the cooked pomegranate juice in a bowl. Add chicken and stir.

7. Place tortilla chips on a serving platter. Top with chicken mixture, pomegranate arils, jalapeño slices, and feta cheese.

8. Serve immediately.

BUTTER CORN KERNELS

Preparation time: 2 minutes

Cooking time: 10 minutes

Number of servings: 2

Ingredients:

- 8 ounces frozen sweet corn kernels
- Salt to taste
- 2 tablespoons butter
- Lemon juice to taste
- Spices and herbs of your choice (optional)

Directions:

1. Pour 1 cup water into the cooking pot in the instant pot.
2. Place a steamer basket in the instant pot and the corn in the basket.
3. Close the lid and lock it by setting the valve to the sealed position.

4. Select the 'Steam' button and set the timer for 10 minutes.

5. When the timer goes off, quickly release the excess pressure.

6. Transfer the corn into a bowl. Add the remaining ingredients and stir.

7. Serve.

GARLIC AND BUTTER MUSHROOMS

Preparation time: 10 minutes

Cooking time: 20 minutes

Number of servings: 8

Ingredients:

- 4 tablespoons olive oil
- 4 tablespoons butter + more to serve
- 1 teaspoon minced fresh thyme or ¼ teaspoon dried thyme
- Salt to taste
- 2 pounds small button mushrooms
- 4 teaspoons minced garlic + more to serve
- A handful fresh parsley, chopped, to garnish

Directions:

1. Select the 'Sauté' button. Add oil. Once the oil is hot enough, place the mushrooms in the pot with the stem side up. Do not disturb the mushrooms and cook until

the underside is golden brown. Cook the mushrooms in batches if required.

2. Add butter, thyme, salt, garlic, and parsley and stir. Press the 'Cancel' button.

3. Close the lid and lock it by setting the valve to the sealed position. Select the 'Manual' button and set the timer for 12 minutes.

4. When the timer goes off, allow the pressure to release naturally for 5 minutes, after which quickly release the excess pressure.

5. Transfer into a bowl. Add some garlic and butter and stir. Taste and add salt if desired. Garnish with parsley.

3-2-1 DIP

Preparation time: 5 minutes

Cooking time: 30 minutes

Number of servings: 8 – 12

Ingredients:

- ½ pound ground Italian sausage, discard casings
- 1 can (10 ounces) Rotel tomatoes
- 2 – 3 tablespoons diced fresh red bell peppers, to garnish (optional)
- 1 ½ blocks (8 ounces each) cream cheese
- A handful fresh cilantro or parsley, to garnish (optional)
- Salt to taste

Directions:

1. Select the 'Sauté' button. Add sausage and cook until done. Press the 'Cancel' button.
2. Stir in cream cheese, Rotel tomatoes, and salt. Close the lid.

3. Select the 'Slow cook' button and set the timer for 30 – 40 minutes. Stir until smooth.

4. Transfer into a bowl. Garnish with red bell peppers and cilantro and serve.

MEDITERRANEAN PIZZA DIP

Preparation time: 10 minutes

Cooking time: 20 minutes

Number of servings: 16

- Ingredients:
- 2 packages cream cheese, cut into cubes, softened
- 2 cups chopped cherry tomatoes
- 1 cup sliced black olives, drained
- 6 ounces feta cheese, crumbled
- 1 tablespoon chopped fresh basil
- 16 ounces Monterey Jack cheese, shredded
- 1 ½ cups chopped, boneless ham steak
- 1 cup canned, marinated artichoke hearts, drained, chopped
- 6 cloves garlic, pressed

Directions:

1. Add all the ingredients into the instant pot pan insert and mix well. Cover the pan with foil.

2. Pour 1 ½ cups water into the cooking pot in the instant pot. Place a trivet in it and set the baking dish on the trivet.

3. Close the lid and lock it by setting the valve to the sealed position. Select the 'Manual' button and set the timer for 10 minutes.

4. When the timer goes off, quickly release the excess pressure.

5. Stir well and serve.

WHITE KIDNEY BEANS/CANNELLINI BEANS DIP

Preparation time: 10 minutes + soaking time

Cooking time: 20 minutes

Number of servings: 20 – 25

Ingredients:

- 2 cups white kidney beans or cannellini beans, soaked in water overnight
- 3 ½ cups water
- 4 cloves roasted garlic
- ½ cup nutritional yeast
- 2 tablespoons lemon juice
- Pepper to taste
- 1 cup coconut yogurt
- 4 tablespoons water or cooked bean water
- Salt to taste

To serve:

- 2 tablespoons extra-virgin olive oil
- Cayenne pepper to taste

- 2 teaspoons fresh or dried parsley leaves

Directions:

1. Add beans and water into the cooking pot in the instant pot.
2. Close the lid and lock it by setting the valve to the sealed position. Select the 'Manual' button and set the timer for 10 minutes.
3. When the timer goes off, allow the pressure to release naturally. Drain off most of the liquid (retain 3 – 4 tablespoons cooked liquid).
4. Add all ingredients in a blender and blend well. Add more water or cooked liquid if desired.
5. Pour into a bowl. Drizzle oil on top. Serve with a garnish of parsley.

HUMMUS

Preparation time: 10 minutes + soaking time

Cooking time: 25 minutes

Number of servings: 6

Ingredients:

- 4 ounces dried chickpeas, soaked in water overnight, drained
- 1 ½ cups water
- 1 teaspoon kosher salt, divided
- ¼ cup tahini
- 2 small cloves garlic, peeled
- 1 tablespoon fresh lemon juice
- Za'atar spice to taste (optional), garnish
- ¼ teaspoon ground cumin
- Sumac to taste (optional), to garnish

Directions:

1. Place drained chickpeas in the cooking pot in the instant pot. Add ½ teaspoon salt, garlic, and water.

2. Close the lid and lock it by setting the valve to the sealed position. Select the 'Beans/Chili' button and set the timer for 25 minutes.

3. When the timer goes off, allow the pressure to release naturally. Drain off most of the liquid (retain 3 – 4 tablespoons cooked liquid).

4. Add chickpeas and rest the ingredients into a blender and blend until nearly smooth or the texture you desire is achieved. Add more water or cooked liquid if needed while blending to get the desired consistency.

5. Pour into a bowl. Drizzle oil on top. Garnish with za'atar and sumac and serve.

6. The leftovers can be stored in the refrigerator for 3 – 4 days in an airtight container.

CHAPTER 4: MEDITERRANEAN DIET SOUP, CHILI, AND STEW RECIPES

CLASSIC MINESTRONE SOUP

Preparation time: 5 minutes

Cooking time: 20 minutes

Number of servings: 4

Ingredients:

- 1 tablespoon olive oil
- 2 cloves garlic, minced

- 1 small carrot, diced
- 2 tomatoes, diced
- Coarsely ground pepper to taste
- 1 rib celery chopped
- 1 small onion, chopped
- 5 – 6 green beans, stringed, chopped into pieces
- ½ cup whole wheat elbow pasta
- ½ can (from a 15 ounce can) kidney beans
- 3 cups chicken broth or water
- Salt to taste
- 1 tablespoon Italian seasoning
- ½ can (from a 14.1 ounce can) crushed tomatoes

Directions

1. Select the 'Sauté' button. Add oil. Once the oil is hot enough, add the onion, garlic, and celery and cook for a couple of minutes.
2. Add the rest of the ingredients except parmesan cheese and stir.
3. Close the lid and lock it by setting the valve to the sealed position. Select the 'Manual' button and set the timer for 4 minutes.

4. When the timer goes off, allow the pressure to release naturally for 5 minutes, after which quickly release the excess pressure.

5. Ladle into soup bowls. Sprinkle parmesan cheese on top and serve.

CHICKEN AND CAULIFLOWER RICE SOUP

Preparation time: 15 minutes

Cooking time: 15 minutes

Number of servings: 8 - 10

Ingredients:

For soup:

- 2 tablespoons olive oil
- 2 pounds chicken breast, cubed
- 4 stalks celery, sliced
- 24 ounces frozen cauliflower rice
- 8 cups chicken broth
- 1 small onion, thinly sliced
- Salt to taste
- 16 ounces baby carrots, halved
- 16 ounces frozen diced sweet potatoes
- A handful fresh cilantro, chopped, to garnish

For spices:

- 2 teaspoons salt
- 4 teaspoons Italian seasoning
- ½ teaspoon ground ginger
- 2 teaspoons turmeric powder
- 1 teaspoon garlic powder
- ½ teaspoon cayenne pepper (optional)

Directions:

1. Add the spices in a bowl and mix well. Keep the spice blend aside.
2. Select the 'Sauté' button. Add oil. Once the oil is hot enough, add the onion and cook until it becomes translucent.
3. Season the chicken with salt and pepper and place in the instant pot. Sear for 3 – 4 minutes on each side.
4. Add spice mixture and mix well. Select the 'Cancel' button.
5. Add the remaining soup ingredients and mix well.
6. Close the lid and lock it by setting the valve to the sealed position.
7. Select the 'Poultry' button.

8. When the timer goes off, quickly release the excess pressure.

9. Add cilantro and stir.

10. Serve hot in soup bowls.

11. Store leftovers in the refrigerator. They will easily last for about 3 – 4 days if stored in an airtight container. It can also be frozen in freezer-safe bags for up to 2 months.

VEGAN CABBAGE DETOX SOUP

Preparation time: 10 minutes

Cooking time: 20 minutes

Number of servings: 3

Ingredients:

- 1 ½ cups chopped green cabbage
- ½ can (from a 14.1 ounce can) diced tomatoes
- 1 ½ medium carrots, chopped
- ½ onion, chopped
- 1 ½ stalks celery, chopped
- 1 clove garlic, sliced
- 1 teaspoon dried sage
- 1 ¼ cups vegetable broth
- 1 tablespoon apple cider vinegar
- Salt to taste
- Pepper to taste

Directions:

1. Add all the ingredients into the cooking pot in the instant pot and stir.

2. Close the lid and lock it by setting the valve to the sealed position. Select the 'Manual' button and set the timer for 10 minutes.

3. When the timer goes off, allow the pressure to release naturally for 10 minutes, and after that quickly release the excess pressure.

4. Serve hot in soup bowls.

RED LENTIL AND YELLOW SPLIT PEA SOUP

Preparation time: 10 minutes

Cooking time: 30 minutes

Number of servings: 5

Ingredients:

- ½ cup yellow split peas, rinsed
- ½ cup red lentils, rinsed
- ½ large onion, chopped
- 3 cloves garlic, chopped
- 4 cups chicken broth
- ½ teaspoon lemon juice or to taste
- 1 carrot, chopped
- Pepper to taste
- ¾ teaspoon ground cumin
- Salt to taste

Directions:

1. Add all the ingredients except lemon juice into the instant pot and stir.

2. Close the lid and lock it by setting the valve to the sealed position. Select the 'Beans/Chili' button.

3. When the timer goes off, allow the pressure to release naturally.

4. Add salt, pepper, and lemon juice and stir.

5. Serve hot in soup bowls.

CHICKEN POSOLE VERDE

Preparation time: 20 minutes

Cooking time: 40 minutes

Number of servings: 4

Ingredients:

- ½ pound tomatillos, husked, chopped
- ½ large jalapeño pepper, deseeded, chopped
- ½ large poblano pepper, deseeded, chopped
- ½ cup fresh cilantro leaves
- 1 clove garlic, minced
- 1 pound skinless, boneless chicken breasts, cut into cubes
- 1 teaspoon Mexican oregano
- 1 ½ cans (15.5 ounces each) white hominy, drained
- Juice of ½ lime
- 1 tablespoon olive oil
- 2 small onions, chopped
- ½ teaspoon ground cumin
- 1 ½ cups chicken broth

- Pepper to taste
- Salt to taste

Directions:

1. To make salsa Verde: Blend together tomatillos, jalapeño, poblano, cilantro, garlic, and lime juice in a blender.
2. Press the 'Sauté' button. Add oil and allow it to heat. Add the onion and chicken and sauté for a couple of minutes.
3. Add cumin and oregano and mix well. Stir in salsa Verde, chicken broth, and hominy. Press the 'Cancel' button.
4. Close the lid and lock it by setting the valve to the sealed position. Select the 'Soup' button.
5. When the timer goes off, allow the pressure to release naturally.
6. Add salt and pepper and stir.
7. Serve hot in soup bowls.

CHICKEN CHILI WITH WHITE BEANS

Preparation time: 15 minutes

Cooking time: 60 minutes

Number of servings: 4

Ingredients:

- 1 tablespoon vegetable oil
- ½ medium onion, diced
- ½ can (from a 28 ounce can) green enchilada sauce
- 1 cup chicken broth
- ½ tablespoon oregano
- ½ cup shredded Monterey Jack cheese blend
- ¾ chicken breast
- 2 cloves garlic, crushed
- 1 cup dry Great Northern beans, picked, rinsed
- 1 can (4 ounces) chopped green chilies with its liquid
- ½ teaspoon ground cumin
- ¼ cup chopped cilantro

Directions:

1. Press the 'Sauté' button. Add oil and allow it to heat. Add chicken and cook until light brown all over.

2. Stir in garlic and onion and cook until the onions turn soft.

3. Pour dry beans, enchilada sauce, green chilies, broth, cumin, and oregano and mix well. Press the 'Cancel' button.

4. Close the lid and lock it by setting the valve to the sealed position. Select the 'Beans/Chili' button.

5. When the timer goes off, allow the pressure to release naturally.

6. Add salt and pepper and stir.

7. Serve hot in soup bowls.

TURKEY CHILI

Preparation time: 15 minutes

Cooking time: 25 minutes

Number of servings: 3

Ingredients:

- ½ tablespoon extra-virgin olive oil
- ½ pound ground turkey
- 4 cloves garlic, sliced or ½ teaspoon garlic powder
- ½ large onion, chopped
- 1 teaspoon ground cumin
- Salt to taste
- ½ red bell pepper, diced
- 1 can beans of your choice or use a mixture of beans, drained
- 1 medium sweet potato, peeled, cut into ½ inch cubes
- ½ can (from a 28 ounce can) crushed tomatoes
- 1 cup chicken broth
- 1 teaspoon ground chipotle chili powder

- Pepper to taste
- ½ tablespoon chili powder

<u>Directions:</u>

1. Select the 'Sauté' button. Add oil. Once the oil is hot enough, add turkey, salt, pepper, fresh garlic, and onion and sauté until it is no longer pink. Break it with the spatula as it cooks.
2. Stir in chili powder, cumin, chipotle chili, and garlic powder if using. Stir-fry for a few seconds until aromatic.
3. Stir in sweet potatoes, tomatoes, bell pepper, and broth and mix well. Press the 'Cancel' button.
4. Close the lid and lock it by setting the valve to the sealed position. Select the 'Manual' button and set the timer for 10 minutes.
5. When the timer goes off, release extra pressure.
6. Serve hot in soup bowls.

ITALIAN BEEF STEW WITH SAGE AND RED WINE

Preparation time: 10 minutes

Cooking time: 25 minutes

Number of servings: 3

Ingredients:

- ½ tablespoon extra-virgin olive oil
- Salt to taste
- ¼ teaspoon sage
- ½ red pepper, chopped
- 1 zucchini, thinly sliced
- ¾ cup water
- ¾ pound stew beef, chopped into bite-size chunks
- ½ teaspoon pepper or to taste
- ½ teaspoon thyme
- 2 small potatoes or 1 large potato, cut into bite-size cubes
- 5 ounces mushroom, quartered
- ¾ cup red wine

Directions:

1. Select the 'Sauté' button. Add oil and allow it to heat. Add beef and cook until brown all over.

2. Stir in remaining ingredients. Press the 'Cancel' button.

3. Close the lid and lock it by setting the valve to the sealed position. Select the 'Meat /Stew' button and set the timer for 20 minutes.

4. When the timer goes off, allow the pressure to release naturally.

5. Serve hot in soup bowls.

MIDDLE EASTERN LAMB STEW

Preparation time: 15 minutes

Cooking time: 60 minutes

Number of servings: 8

Ingredients:

- 4 tablespoons olive oil
- 2 onions, diced
- 3 – 3 ½ pounds lamb stew meat, cut into bite-size chunks
- 8 – 12 cloves garlic, chopped
- 4 tablespoons tomato paste
- 4 tablespoons honey
- 2 cans (15 ounces each) chickpeas, rinsed, drained
- ½ cup raisins or dried, chopped apricots

For spices:

- 2 teaspoons salt or to taste
- 2 teaspoons ground cumin
- 2 teaspoons turmeric powder

- 2 teaspoons cumin seeds
- 2 teaspoons pepper
- 2 teaspoons ground coriander
- 2 teaspoons ground cinnamon
- 1 teaspoon chili flakes
- Cilantro, to garnish

<u>To serve: Use any</u>

- Cooked quinoa
- Cooked couscous
- Cooked basmati rice

Directions:

1. Select the 'Sauté' button. Add oil and allow it to heat. Add the onion and cook for a couple of minutes until translucent.

2. Stir in lamb, salt, garlic, and all the spices. Cook for about 5 minutes.

3. Stir in the rest of the ingredients. Press the 'Cancel' button.

4. Close the lid and lock it by setting the valve to the sealed position. Select the 'Meat/Stew' button and set the timer for 20 minutes.

5. When the timer goes off, allow the pressure to release naturally. The meat should almost fall off the bones.

6. Mix well. Garnish with cilantro and serve with any of the suggested serving options.

BRAZILIAN FISH STEW

Preparation time: 15 minutes

Cooking time: 40 minutes

Number of servings: 10

Ingredients:

For stew base:

- 2 onions, finely chopped
- 10 cloves garlic, peeled, minced
- 2 cups seafood or fish broth
- 4 tablespoons olive oil
- 2 tablespoons smoked paprika
- 1 teaspoon pepper or to taste
- 2 tablespoons ground cumin
- 2 teaspoons salt or to taste
- ½ teaspoon cayenne pepper
- 2 red bell peppers, sliced
- 2 cans (14 ounces each) crushed tomatoes

- 1 ½ cups canned coconut milk

Other ingredients:

- 3 pounds fresh or frozen white fish, thaw if frozen, discard skin and bones
- 2 tablespoons fresh lime juice
- 4 tablespoons olive oil
- 2 tablespoons chopped fresh cilantro or parsley

Directions:

1. Place all the stew base ingredients into the cooking pot in the instant pot and mix well.
2. Close the lid and lock it by setting the valve to the sealed position. Select the 'Manual' button and set the timer for 10 minutes.
3. When the timer goes off, allow the pressure to release naturally for 10 minutes, and after that quickly release the excess pressure.
4. Meanwhile, dry the fish with paper towels and chop into 1 inch chunks.
5. Open the lid. Select the 'Sauté' button. Let the stew simmer until slightly thick.
6. Add fish and stir. Simmer until the fish cooks. Check the fish by piercing with a fork. If it flakes readily, the

fish is cooked. If not, continue cooking for a few more minutes.

7. Press the 'Cancel' button. Add oil and lime juice and stir.

8. Serve in bowls with cilantro garnished on top.

9. Transfer extra stew into airtight containers and refrigerate. It can be stored for 3 days.

MEDITERRANEAN CHICKEN AND QUINOA STEW

Preparation time: 15 minutes

Cooking time: 20 – 25 minutes

Number of servings: 3

Ingredients:

- 10 ounces boneless, skinless chicken thighs
- 2 cups chicken stock
- 1 clove garlic, sliced
- Salt to taste
- ½ teaspoon ground fennel seeds
- ¼ cup uncooked quinoa, rinsed
- 2 cups peeled, chopped, butternut squash
- ½ cup chopped yellow onion
- 2 small bay leaves
- ½ teaspoon dried oregano
- Pepper to taste
- ½ ounce pitted Castelvetrano olives, sliced

Directions:

1. Add chicken, stock, garlic, salt, squash, bay leaves, oregano, pepper, and fennel into the cooking pot in the instant pot.

2. Close the lid and lock it by setting the valve to the sealed position. Select the 'Manual' button and set the timer for 8 minutes.

3. When the timer goes off, allow the pressure to release naturally.

4. Take the chicken out of the instant pot and place it on the cutting board. Once cooled enough to handle comfortably, shred the chicken.

5. Meanwhile, add quinoa into the pot. Select the 'Sauté' button and simmer until the quinoa is cooked.

6. Add chicken and stir. Ladle into soup bowls. Garnish with olives and serve.

AFRICAN CHICKEN AND PEANUT STEW

Preparation time: 15 minutes

Cooking time: 13 minutes

Number of servings: 8

Ingredients:

- 3 carrots, coarsely chopped
- ½ large sweet onion, coarsely chopped
- 1 ½ green bell peppers, coarsely chopped
- ½ jalapeño pepper, coarsely chopped
- 2 cups chicken broth
- ½ can (from a 12 ounce can) tomato paste
- ½ can (from a 14 ounce can) diced tomatoes
- ¼ teaspoon garlic powder
- Salt to taste
- Cayenne pepper to taste
- Pepper to taste
- 1 pound skinless, boneless chicken thighs
- ½ cup peanut butter

- A handful fresh cilantro, chopped, to garnish
- Salted, roasted peanuts, to serve, coarsely chopped
- Hot cooked brown rice, to serve

Directions:

1. Add all the vegetables and about 1/3 cup water into the cooking pot in the instant pot.
2. Close the lid and lock it by setting the valve to the sealed position. Select the 'Manual' button and set the timer for 8 minutes.
3. When the timer goes off, allow the pressure to release naturally for 5 minutes, after which release extra pressure.
4. Blend with a stick blender until smooth.
5. Add broth, tomato paste, tomatoes, spices, and salt. Stir well.
6. Close the lid and lock it by setting the valve to the sealed position. Select the 'Manual' button and set the timer for 13 minutes.
7. When the timer goes off, release the extra pressure.
8. Take out the chicken and transfer it to the cutting board. Once cooled enough to touch, shred with a fork.

9. Add the chicken back into the pot. Add peanut butter and stir.//
10. Serve rice on the plates. Ladle the stew over the rice. Garnish with cilantro and peanuts and serve.

CHAPTER 5:
MEDITERRANEAN DIET SALAD RECIPES

SALAD NICOISE

Preparation time: 35 minutes

Cooking time: 8 minutes

Number of servings: 4

Ingredients:

For salad:

- 4 large Yukon gold potatoes, peeled, cut into 1 ½ inch cubes

- 4 large eggs
- 1 can tuna
- 2 – 4 small beets, peeled, cut into 1-inch cubes
- 2 handfuls snap peas or string beans, trimmed, discard strings
- 15 – 20 cherry tomatoes or grape tomatoes
- Olive oil to drizzle
- 2 – 3 teaspoons vinegar
- Lettuce leaves to serve

Directions:

1. Spread potatoes and beet in the cooking pot in the instant pot. Place eggs over them.
2. Place snap peas on a sheet of foil and wrap it on 3 sides, leaving one side open.
3. Pour a cup of water into the pot.
4. Close the lid and lock it by setting the valve to the sealed position. Select the 'Manual' button and set the timer for 3 minutes.
5. When the timer goes off, allow the pressure to release naturally for 2 minutes, after which quickly release the excess pressure.

6. Lift the eggs with a spoon and place in a bowl of cold water. When they are cool enough to handle, peel the eggs and cut into cubes.

7. Drain off the water from the pot. Transfer the vegetables onto a bowl. Drizzle oil and vinegar over it and toss well.

8. Serve salad over a bed of lettuce leaves.

CRUNCHY NOODLE SALAD

Preparation time: 10 minutes

Cooking time: 10 minutes

Number of servings: 3

Ingredients:

For salad:

- ½ pound thin spaghetti
- 1 ½ large carrots, shredded
- ½ cup bean sprouts
- ½ pound sugar snap peas, trim ends
- 1 scallion, sliced
- ½ red bell pepper, deseeded, sliced

For dressing:

- 2 tablespoons vegetable oil
- 3 tablespoons soy sauce
- 1½ tablespoon honey
- 1 teaspoon grated fresh ginger

- 2 tablespoons rice wine vinegar
- 1 ½ tablespoons sesame oil
- 1 clove garlic, peeled, grated
- 6 tablespoons crunchy peanut butter
- A handful roasted peanuts or almonds, chopped to garnish
- Cilantro leaves to garnish

Directions:

1. Add spaghetti and 2 cups of water into the cooking pot in the instant pot.
2. Close the lid and lock it by setting the valve to the sealed position. Select the 'Manual' button and set the timer for 4 minutes.
3. When the timer goes off, quickly release the excess pressure.
4. Rinse the spaghetti under cold running water and drain well.
5. Add sugar snap peas to the instant pot and ¼ cup water.
6. Close the lid and lock it by setting the valve to the sealed position.

7. Select the 'Steam' button and set the timer for 3 minutes. Quickly release the excess pressure. Drain and add into the bowl of noodles. Also add scallion, carrot, and bell pepper and toss well.

8. To make the dressing: Whisk together all the ingredients for dressing in a small bowl and pour over the salad.

9. Toss well. Garnish with peanuts and cilantro and serve.

WARM WHITE BEAN SALAD

Preparation time: 10 minutes

Cooking time: 12 minutes

Number of servings: 3

Ingredients:

- ¾ cup dried cannellini or Great Northern beans, rinsed, soaked in water overnight, drained
- 2 ½ tablespoons olive oil
- ¼ cup chopped red onion
- 1 teaspoon minced garlic
- 1 teaspoon finely chopped rosemary leaves
- 1/8 teaspoon red pepper flakes
- Water, as required
- 1 tablespoon white wine vinegar
- 2 tablespoons chopped fresh parsley
- 1 teaspoon drained, rinsed, finely chopped capers
- Salt to taste

Directions:

1. Place beans in the cooking pot in the instant pot. Pour enough water to cover the beans and about 2 inches above the beans.

2. Add ½ tablespoon oil and stir.

3. Close the lid and lock it by setting the valve to the sealed position. Select the 'Manual' button and set the timer for 3 minutes.

4. When the timer goes off, allow the pressure to release naturally.

5. Drain and add beans into a bowl.

6. Add oil and vinegar into another bowl and whisk it well. Add the onion, garlic, parsley, rosemary, capers, red pepper flakes, and salt and toss well.

TUNA PASTA SALAD

Preparation time: 5 minutes

Cooking time: 4 minutes

Number of servings: 3

Ingredients:

- ½ pound whole wheat penne pasta or fusilli pasta
- Salt to taste
- ½ cup sweet corn kernels
- ½ can (from a 24 ounce can) tuna, drained
- ½ teaspoon chopped dill, preferably fresh
- 2 cups water
- ½ cup chopped olives
- ½ cup chopped sun-dried tomatoes
- Balsamic vinaigrette to taste

Directions:

1. Place pasta into the cooking pot in the instant pot. Pour water.

2. Close the lid and lock it by setting the valve to the sealed position. Select the 'Manual' button and set the timer for 4 minutes.

3. When the timer goes off, allow the pressure to release naturally for 3 minutes, after which quickly release the excess pressure.

4. Drain and add the pasta into a bowl. Add the rest of the ingredients and toss well.

5. Serve.

AVOCADO EGG SALAD

Preparation time: 20 minutes

Cooking time: 5 minutes

Number of servings: 3

Ingredients:

- 3 eggs

For dressing:

- ½ teaspoon Dijon mustard
- 1 tablespoon avocado oil mayonnaise
- 1 tablespoon chopped herbs of your choice like chives, dill, cilantro, etc.
- Freshly ground black pepper
- ½ tablespoon fresh lemon juice
- Salt to taste
- ½ tablespoon minced red onion
- ½ ripe avocado, peeled, pitted, mashed

Directions:

1. Pour 1 cup water into the cooking pot in the instant pot. Place a trivet or steamer basket in it.
2. Place the eggs on it.
3. Close the lid and lock it by setting the valve to the sealed position. Select the 'Manual' button and set the timer for 5 minutes.
4. When the timer goes off, quickly release the excess pressure.
5. Meanwhile, add all the dressing ingredients into a bowl and mix them well.
6. Remove the eggs and place in a bowl of cold water for a while. Peel the eggs.
7. Chop the eggs into bite-size pieces and add them into a bowl.
8. Add the dressing and fold gently.
9. Serve.

INSTANT POT BEET SALAD WITH YOGURT, LIME & JALAPEÑO

Preparation time: 10 minutes

Cooking time: 30 minutes

Number of servings: 2

Ingredients:

- 3 medium beets, scrubbed, trimmed
- ½ cup plain Greek yogurt
- 1 tablespoon chopped cilantro
- Salt to taste
- Flaky salt to garnish
- Pepper to taste
- Zest of ½ lime
- 2 small cloves garlic, finely grated
- ½ jalapeño, deseeded, thinly sliced
- Olive oil, to drizzle

Directions:

1. Pour a cup of water into the cooking pot in the instant pot. Place a trivet in the instant pot and the beets on the trivet.

2. Close the lid and lock it by setting the valve to the sealed position. Select the 'Manual' button and set the timer for 5 minutes.

3. When the timer goes off, allow the pressure to release naturally. If the beets are not cooked, cook for another 5 – 8 minutes.

4. Remove the beets and let them cool till comfortable to touch. Peel the beets and cut into cubes. Place in a bowl. Pour olive oil on top and toss well.

5. Whisk yogurt, lime juice, salt, pepper, lime zest, and garlic in a bowl.

6. Divide beets, jalapeño, and cilantro into 2 plates. Scatter flaky salt on top. Place yogurt mixture on the sides of the plate and serve.

CHICKEN BACON AVOCADO SALAD

Preparation time: 10 minutes

Cooking time: 10 minutes

Number of servings: 3

Ingredients:

For salad:

- 1 boneless, skinless chicken breast
- ¾ cup chicken broth
- 3 ounces bacon, cooked, crumbled
- 1 medium tomato, diced
- Salt to taste
- 1 egg
- 1 cup frozen white sweet corn kernels
- 1 green onion, sliced
- 1 large ripe avocado, peeled, pitted, cut into chunks
- Freshly ground pepper to taste

For dressing:

- Juice of ½ lemon
- Salt to taste
- ½ teaspoon dried dill
- 1 ½ tablespoons extra-virgin olive oil
- Pepper to taste

Directions:

1. Add broth into the cooking pot in the instant pot. For fresh chicken, place the chicken directly in the pot. Place the egg in a heatproof container on top of the chicken. For frozen chicken, place chicken on a trivet or rack in the pot and place the egg on the rack as well.

2. Close the lid and lock it by setting the valve to the sealed position. Select the 'Manual' button and set the timer for 10 minutes.

3. When the timer goes off, allow the pressure to release naturally for about 9 – 10 minutes, after which quickly release the excess pressure.

4. Meanwhile, whisk together all the ingredients for dressing in a bowl.

5. Take out the chicken and transfer it to the cutting board. Once cool enough to handle, shred or chop the chicken.

6. Peel and cut the egg into pieces.

7. Add chicken, egg, and the other ingredients in a bowl and toss to mix.

8. Pour dressing on top and toss once again.

9. Cover and set aside for a few minutes so that the flavors blend together.

CHAPTER 6:
MEDITERRANEAN DIET LUNCH RECIPES

MEDITERRANEAN SPINACH-FETA PIE

Preparation time: 25 minutes

Cooking time: 30 minutes

Number of servings: 4

Ingredients:

- 1 ½ tablespoons butter or ghee + extra to grease
- 3 cloves garlic, peeled, grated
- 2 eggs
- Salt to taste
- 3 tablespoons chopped Italian parsley
- A large pinch freshly grated ground nutmeg
- 1 cup crumbled feta cheese
- ½ medium onion, chopped
- 1 pound spinach, chopped

- 1/3 cup heavy cream
- Zest of ½ lemon, grated
- 1 ½ tablespoons chopped fresh dill
- 1/3 cup shredded Parmigiano Reggiano cheese
- 1 cup water

Directions:

1. Select the 'Sauté' button. Add butter and let it melt. Add garlic and onion and cook until light brown.
2. Add the spinach and cook for a few minutes until it wilts. Select the 'Cancel' button.
3. Grease a heatproof dish or instant pot pan insert accessory, which can easily fit into the instant pot, with some butter.
4. Beat eggs in a bowl. Add cream and whisk it well. Add lemon zest, dill, salt, parsley, and nutmeg and whisk lightly until well incorporated.
5. Add Parmigiano Reggiano cheese and onion mixture and stir.
6. Spoon the mixture into the prepared pan. Scatter feta cheese on top. Cover with a lid or foil.
7. Pour a cup of water into the cooking pot in the instant pot.

8. Place a trivet in the pot and the dish on the trivet.

9. Close the lid and lock it by setting the valve to the sealed position. Select the 'Manual' button and set the timer for 20 minutes.

10. When the timer goes off, allow the pressure to release naturally for about 9 – 10 minutes, after which quickly release the excess pressure.

11. Cool for a few minutes. Slice into wedges and serve.

GREEK CHICKEN TACOS

Preparation time: 20 minutes

Cooking time: 8 minutes

Number of servings: 4

Ingredients:

For chicken filling:

- 2 large chicken breasts, skinless, boneless, cut into strips lengthwise
- ½ tablespoon Greek seasoning
- 2 tablespoons chicken stock
- Freshly ground pepper to taste
- Zest of a lemon, grated
- Juice of a lemon
- 1 tablespoon extra-virgin olive oil
- ¼ teaspoon Greek oregano

For Greek salsa:

- 3 small cucumbers, peeled, chopped

- 2 tablespoons chopped kalamata olives
- 2 ounces crumbled feta cheese
- ½ cup chopped cherry tomatoes
- 2 tablespoons finely chopped red onion
- 2 tablespoons low-sugar Italian dressing of your choice

<u>*To serve:*</u>

- 2 whole wheat tortillas or any other low carb tortillas of your choice

Directions:

1. Place chicken in the cooking pot in the instant pot.
2. Add lemon juice, lemon zest, oil, oregano, Greek seasoning, chicken stock, and pepper into a bowl and whisk it well.
3. Drizzle this mixture over the chicken.
4. Close the lid and lock it by setting the valve to the sealed position. Select the 'Manual' button and set the timer for 8 minutes.
5. When the timer goes off, allow the pressure to release naturally for about 9 – 10 minutes, after which quickly release the excess pressure.
6. To make the salsa: Add all the ingredients for salsa into a bowl and stir gently until well combined.

7. To assemble: Warm the tortillas following the directions on the package.

8. Divide the chicken filling among the tortillas. Drizzle some salsa on it. Fold and serve.

GROUND TURKEY QUINOA BOWLS

Preparation time: 10 minutes

Cooking time: 20 minutes

Number of servings: 3

Ingredients:

- ½ pound ground turkey or chicken or beef
- ½ teaspoon taco seasoning
- Salt to taste
- ½ tablespoon oil
- ½ teaspoon dried oregano
- Pepper to taste
- ¾ cup uncooked quinoa, rinsed
- 2 cloves garlic, peeled, grated
- 1 tablespoon soy sauce
- 1 cup frozen green peas
- 1 green onion, thinly sliced
- ¾ cup water
- ½ large onion, chopped

- ½ bell pepper, finely chopped
- 1 tablespoon maple syrup or honey
- 1 cup frozen corn kernels

Directions:

1. Select the 'Sauté' button. Add oil to the pot and allow it to heat. Add turkey and cook until it is not pink anymore.
2. Stir in oregano, taco seasoning, pepper, salt, and water. Scrape the base of the pot to remove any browned bits that have become stuck. Select the 'Cancel' button.
3. Stir in quinoa, onion, bell pepper, maple syrup, and soy sauce.
4. Close the lid and lock it by setting the valve to the sealed position. Select the 'Manual' button and set it on low pressure. Set the timer for 10 minutes.
5. When the timer goes off, quickly release the excess pressure.
6. Stir in peas and corn. Cover and let it sit for 5 minutes.
7. Stir in green onion and serve.

BLACK EYED PEAS WITH FRESH DILL AND PARSLEY

Preparation time: 10 minutes

Cooking time: 25 minutes

Number of servings: 3

Ingredients:

- 1 cup dried black-eyed beans, rinsed
- ½ cup chopped parsley leaves
- 2 green onions, thinly sliced
- ½ cup chopped dill leaves
- 1 carrot, peeled, sliced
- 1 orange slice along with peel
- Salt to taste
- ½ cup extra-virgin olive oil
- 1 bay leaf
- 1 tablespoon tomato paste
- 1 ½ cups water

Directions:

1. Place all the ingredients in the cooking pot in the instant pot and mix well.

2. Close the lid and lock it by setting the valve to the sealed position. Select the 'Manual' button and set the timer for 8 minutes.

3. When the timer goes off, allow the pressure to release naturally.

4. Stir and serve as it is or over cooked brown rice or quinoa.

ACORN SQUASH STUFFED WITH CRANBERRIES, WILD RICE, AND CHICKPEAS

Preparation time: 15 minutes

Cooking time: 55 minutes

Number of servings: 4

Ingredients:

- 1/3 cup uncooked wild rice
- 2 small acorn squashes, halved lengthwise, trimmed, deseeded
- ½ medium shallot, finely chopped
- 4 ounces baby Bella mushrooms, finely chopped
- ½ can (from a 15 ounce can) chickpeas
- 2 tablespoons toasted pepitas or chopped pecans
- Salt to taste
- ½ tablespoon oil
- 2 large cloves garlic, peeled, minced
- Pepper to taste
- Water, as required

Directions:

1. Add about a cup of water into the cooking pot in the instant pot. Place a steamer basket in it. Place the squash on it, with the skin side touching the basket.

2. Cook in batches if required.

3. Close the lid and lock it by setting the valve to the sealed position. Select the 'Manual' button and set the timer for 4 minutes.

4. When the timer goes off, allow the pressure to release naturally for 5 minutes, after which remove extra pressure. Drain the water from the pot.

5. To make wild rice: Add wild rice, ¼ teaspoon salt, and ¾ cup water into the cooking pot in the instant pot.

6. Close the lid and lock it by setting the valve to the sealed position. Select the 'Multigrain' button and set the timer for 20 minutes.

7. When the timer goes off, allow the pressure to release naturally for 5 minutes and then release extra pressure.

8. Fluff rice with a fork.

9. Place the acorn squash halves on a baking sheet, with the base facing down.

10. Place a skillet over medium heat. Add oil and once the oil is hot enough, add the shallots and cook until translucent.

11. Stir in garlic and cook for a few seconds until aromatic. Stir in mushrooms, salt, and pepper and cook until tender.

12. Stir in chickpeas, thyme, pepitas, cranberries, and wild rice and mix well. Add salt if desired.

13. Fill the chickpea mixture into the squash halves and serve.

SPANISH CHICKEN AND RICE

Preparation time: 15 minutes

Cooking time: 40 minutes

Number of servings: 3

Ingredients:

- ¾ pound bone-in skin-on chicken thighs
- 1 tablespoon olive oil
- ¼ onion, sliced
- ½ teaspoon ground red pepper
- ¼ teaspoon white pepper
- ½ pound tomatoes, diced
- ½ cup long-grain brown rice
- Salt to taste
- ½ red bell pepper, diced
- 2 cloves garlic, minced
- ½ teaspoon ground cumin
- ½ teaspoon dried oregano
- Red pepper flakes to taste

- ¾ cup chicken broth
- ½ cup frozen peas, partially thawed

Directions:

1. Sprinkle salt over the chicken and rub the salt into the chicken thoroughly.
2. Press the 'Sauté' button. Add oil and allow it to heat.
3. Add the chicken and cook until brown all over while stirring. Remove chicken from the pan and set aside on a plate.
4. Add the onion, bell pepper, and garlic into the cooking pot. Cook for about a minute.
5. Stir in spices and salt and cook for a couple of minutes.
6. Stir in broth and tomatoes. Add rice and stir. Press the 'Cancel' button.
7. Place chicken on top.
8. Close the lid and lock it by setting the valve to the sealed position. Select the 'Rice' button.
9. When the timer goes off, uncover. Add peas and stir lightly.
10. Close the lid and let the rice rest for 10 minutes.
11. Serve hot.

ITALIAN CHICKEN AND BROCCOLI BOWLS

Preparation time: 10 minutes

Cooking time: 3 hours 30 minutes

Number of servings: 2 – 3

Ingredients:

- 1 cup chicken broth
- ½ cup water
- 1 clove garlic, peeled, minced
- Salt to taste
- ½ pound boneless, skinless chicken thighs, chopped into bite-size chunks
- ¾ cup long-grain brown rice
- ½ medium onion, diced
- ½ teaspoon dried Italian herb blend
- ¼ teaspoon red pepper flakes (optional)
- ½ can (from a 15 ounce can) cannellini beans, drained, rinsed
- 6 ounces broccoli, cut into florets

- ¼ cup grated parmesan cheese + extra to serve

Directions:

1. Add rice, broth, water, garlic, onion, Italian herb blend, red pepper flakes, and about ½ teaspoon salt into the instant pot and stir.

2. Add the chicken on top of the rice in an even layer, season with salt to taste.

3. Close the lid and lock it by setting the valve to the sealed position. Select the 'Slow cook' button and adjust to 'Low temperature'. Set the timer for 2 hours.

4. When the timer goes off, remove the lid. Add beans and cheese and stir. Spread the broccoli evenly on top.

5. Close the lid and lock it by setting the valve to the sealed position. Select the 'Slow cook' button and adjust to 'Low temperature'. Set the timer for 90 minutes or until rice is cooked.

6. Stir lightly.

7. Divide into 2 – 3 bowls.

8. Garnish with parmesan cheese and serve.

TURKEY BOLOGNESE

Preparation time: 10 minutes

Cooking time: 30 minutes

Number of servings: 3

Ingredients:

- 1 tablespoon extra-virgin olive oil
- 1 stalk celery, finely chopped
- 1 carrot, finely chopped
- ½ medium onion, finely chopped
- 5 ounces mushrooms, trim the ends, finely chopped

- ½ teaspoon dried thyme
- ¾ teaspoon pepper or to taste
- 2 small bay leaves
- ½ teaspoons sea salt or to taste
- Fresh basil leaves (3 – 4 leaves), chopped
- ½ can (from a 28 ounce can) tomatoes, crushed
- ½ pound ground 93% lean turkey
- 1 clove garlic, minced
- ¼ teaspoon crushed red pepper flakes or to taste
- ¼ cup red wine or chicken stock
- Whole wheat pasta, cooked, to serve

Directions:

1. Press the 'Sauté' feature. Add oil and allow it to heat. Add all the vegetables and cook until the onion turns brown.
2. Stir in turkey and cook until it is no longer pink. Break it as it cooks.
3. Pour red wine and let it cook until it has reduced to half its original volume.
4. Stir in tomatoes, bay leaves, thyme salt, and pepper. Press the 'Cancel' button.

5. Close the lid and lock it by setting the valve to the sealed position. Select the 'Poultry' button and set the timer for 15 minutes.

6. When the timer goes off, allow the pressure to release naturally for 10 minutes, after which release remaining pressure.

7. Add basil leaves. Stir well and cover for a few minutes.

8. Serve over hot cooked whole wheat pasta.

CHAPTER 7:
MEDITERRANEAN DIET POULTRY RECIPES

SPICY CHICKEN SHAWARMA

Preparation time: 10 minutes

Cooking time: 30 minutes

Number of servings: 4 – 6

Ingredients:

- 1 teaspoon salt or to taste
- 2 – 3 pounds skinless, boneless, chicken breast and thighs, thinly sliced into strips
- ½ teaspoon crushed red pepper
- ½ teaspoon paprika
- ½ teaspoon ground cumin
- ¼ teaspoon turmeric powder
- 1/8 teaspoon granulated garlic
- 1/8 ground allspice
- ½ cup chicken stock or broth

- Freshly ground pepper to taste

To serve:

- 2 tablespoons tahini sauce
- 1/3 cup plain low-fat Greek-style yogurt
- 2 garlic cloves, minced
- 4 – 6 (6-inch each) pitas, halved
- Vegetables of your choice to top
- ¼ cup fresh parsley, finely chopped
- 1 tablespoon lemon juice

Directions

1. Add salt and all the spices into a bowl and stir.
2. Add chicken into the instant pot. Sprinkle spice mixture all over the chicken. Stir to coat the chicken well.
3. Close the lid and lock it by setting the valve to the sealed position. Select the 'Poultry' button and set the timer for 15 minutes.
4. When the timer goes off, allow the pressure to release naturally for 10 minutes, after which release the remaining pressure.

5. Meanwhile, add the lemon juice, remaining yogurt, garlic, and tahini into a bowl and mix well. Apply this mixture inside the halved pita bread.

6. Divide the chicken and fill each pita half with chicken mixture. Top the chicken with vegetables of your choice like tomato, cucumber, onions, etc. Serve and enjoy.

TUSCAN CHICKEN

Preparation time: 5 minutes

Cooking time: 15 minutes

Number of servings: 6

Ingredients:

- 2 cups rice
- 2/3 cup basil pesto
- 1 cup sundried tomatoes in oil
- 2 tablespoons Italian seasoning
- 3 cups chicken broth
- 6 boneless, skinless chicken breasts
- 1 cup chopped marinated artichoke hearts in oil, discard the oil
- 2 cups mozzarella cheese

Directions:

1. Place rice in the cooking pot in the instant pot. Pour broth into it. Place chicken over the rice.

2. Spoon pesto over the chicken. Next layer with artichoke hearts followed by ½ cup sundried tomatoes. Next layer with cheese followed by the remaining tomatoes.

3. Sprinkle Italian seasoning on top.

4. Close the lid and lock it by setting the valve to the sealed position. Select the 'Poultry' button and set the timer for 15 minutes.

5. When the timer goes off, allow the pressure to release naturally for 10 minutes, after which release the remaining pressure.

6. Stir and serve.

CAPRESE CHICKEN THIGHS

Preparation time: 10 minutes

Cooking time: 20 minutes

Number of servings: 3

Ingredients:

- 2 tablespoons chicken stock
- 2 tablespoons maple syrup
- 4 slices mozzarella cheese
- ¼ cup torn basil leaves
- 2 tablespoons balsamic vinegar
- ¾ pound boneless skinless chicken thighs
- 1 ½ cups halved cherry tomatoes

Directions:

1. Add stock, maple syrup, and balsamic vinegar into the cooking pot of the instant pot.
2. Stir in the chicken.

3. Close the lid and lock it by setting the valve to the sealed position. Select the 'Manual' button and set the timer for 10 minutes.

4. When the timer goes off, quickly release remaining pressure.

5. Remove the chicken from the pot and place on a baking sheet. Lay a cheese slice on each piece of chicken.

6. Place the baking sheet in a preheated oven and broil for about 3 minutes.

7. Meanwhile, select the 'Sauté' button. Simmer until the gravy has thickened.

8. Add tomatoes and cook for a few minutes until slightly soft. Add basil and stir.

9. Serve chicken with gravy.

CHICKEN CACCIATORE

Preparation time: 15 minutes

Cooking time: 40 minutes

Number of servings: 8

Ingredients:

- 8 bone-in chicken thighs along with skin (6 ounces each)
- 6 stalks celery, chopped
- 2 packages (4 ounces each) mushrooms, sliced
- 2 cans (14 ounces each) stewed tomatoes
- 1 ½ cups water
- 4 tablespoons tomato paste
- Pepper to taste
- 4 tablespoons olive oil
- 1 onion, chopped
- 4 cloves garlic, minced
- 4 teaspoons herbes de Provence
- 6 chicken bouillon cubes, crumbled
- Red pepper flakes to taste
- Salt to taste

Directions:

1. Dry the chicken by patting with paper towels.
2. Select the 'Sauté' button. Add oil. Once the oil is hot enough, add chicken and cook until brown all over.
3. Remove chicken with tongs and set it aside.
4. Add the onion, celery, and mushroom and cook until lightly tender.
5. Stir in garlic and cook until aromatic.
6. Add chicken, tomato paste, and tomatoes and mix well. Stir in herbes de Provence.
7. Add water and bouillon cubes. Press the 'Cancel' button.
8. Close the lid and lock it by setting the valve to the sealed position. Select the 'Manual' button and set the timer for 11 minutes.
9. When the timer goes off, quickly release the remaining pressure.
10. Add salt, pepper, and red pepper flakes to taste and stir. Then serve.

JAMBALAYA

Preparation time: 20 minutes

Cooking time: 20 minutes

Number of servings: 3 – 4

Ingredients:

- ¾ cup boneless skinless chicken thighs, cut into bite-size pieces
- 1 large onion, chopped
- 1 teaspoon Cajun or Creole seasoning
- Salt to taste
- 1 cup chicken broth
- ½ pound peeled, deveined medium shrimp
- 1 green onion, thinly sliced, to garnish
- A handful fresh parsley, chopped
- ½ cup sliced celery
- ½ red bell pepper, diced
- 1 teaspoon minced garlic

- ½ can (from a 14.5 ounce can) diced tomatoes with its liquid
- 3 tablespoons tomato paste
- ½ tablespoon olive oil
- Cooked brown rice, to serve

Directions:

1. Select the 'Sauté' button. Add oil. Once the oil is hot enough, add chicken and cook until brown all over. Remove chicken and set it aside.
2. Stir in Cajun seasoning, onion, celery, and bell pepper and cook until lightly tender.
3. Stir in garlic and cook until aromatic.
4. Add chicken and tomatoes and mix well.
5. Press the 'Cancel' button.
6. Add ½ cup broth and tomato paste and mix well.
7. Close the lid and lock it by setting the valve to the sealed position. Select the 'Manual' button and set the timer for 10 minutes.
8. When the timer goes off, quickly release remaining pressure.
9. Press the 'Sauté' button. Stir in shrimp and simmer until shrimp turns pink. Press the 'Cancel' button.

10. Divide rice into individual serving plates. Top with jambalaya. Sprinkle green onion and parsley on top and serve.

SPICY MEDITERRANEAN CHICKEN

Preparation time: 10 minutes

Cooking time: 30 minutes

Number of servings: 8

Ingredients:

- 2 containers (8 ounces each) zhoug sauce
- 2 jars (12 ounces each) jumbo pitted kalamata olives, drained
- 2 jars fire-roasted red and yellow peppers, drained cut into bite-size pieces
- 8 boneless skinless chicken breasts
- Cooked brown rice or whole grain orzo pasta
- 1 cup water

Directions:

1. Spread half the zhoug sauce on the bottom of the cooking pot in the instant pot.
2. Spread the chicken in the pot. Layer with roasted peppers and olives.

3. Spread remaining zhoug sauce over the chicken. Pour water on and around the chicken.

4. Close the lid and lock it by setting the valve to sealed position. Select the 'Poultry' button and set the timer for 15 minutes.

5. When the timer goes off, allow the pressure to release naturally for 10 minutes, after which quickly release the remaining pressure.

6. Serve hot over rice or orzo.

TURKEY MEATBALLS AND SPAGHETTI SQUASH

Preparation time: 15 minutes

Cooking time: 25 minutes

Number of servings: 10 – 12

Ingredients:

- 2 pounds ground turkey
- 2 eggs
- 1 cup ricotta cheese
- 2 teaspoons dried oregano
- 1 teaspoon crushed red pepper flakes
- 4 tablespoons extra-virgin olive oil
- ½ cup red wine
- 2 parmesan rinds
- Grated parmesan to garnish
- 4 slices thick, soft, whole grain bread
- 10 cloves minced or grated
- 6 ounces prosciutto, diced
- 1 teaspoon ground cumin

- Salt to taste
- 4 cans (28 ounces each) crushed San Marzano tomatoes
- 2 small spaghetti squash
- 4 sprigs fresh thyme
- Pepper to taste
- 1 cup water

Directions:

1. Dip bread slices in a bowl of water and take them out immediately. Squeeze out the extra moisture.
2. Place bread, turkey, ricotta, oregano, eggs, 4 cloves garlic, red pepper flakes, pepper, salt, and cumin into a bowl and mix until well combined.
3. Grease your hands with some oil. Make meatballs out of the mixture and place on a baking sheet.
4. Set an oven on broil mode. Place the baking sheet in the oven and broil for a few minutes until brown.
5. Meanwhile, add red wine, the rest of the garlic, salt, pepper, and water into the cooking pot in the instant pot. Mix well.
6. Pierce spaghetti squash at different places with a fork. Make sure to do this all over the squash.

7. Place the squash in the pot. Place meatballs in the remaining space.

8. Sprinkle thyme and place the parmesan rinds.

9. Close the lid and lock it by setting the valve to the sealed position. Select the 'Poultry' button and set the timer for 30 minutes.

10. When the timer goes off, allow the pressure to release naturally for 10 minutes, after which release the remaining pressure.

11. Discard parmesan rinds.

12. Place the squash on your cutting board. When it is cool enough to handle, cut each into 2 halves. Discard the seeds and shred the squash.

13. Serve meatballs over squash. Drizzle sauce on top. Garnish with basil and parmesan cheese and serve.

ENCHILADA PASTA

Preparation time: 20 minutes

Cooking time: 10 minutes

Number of servings: 8

Ingredients:

- 16 ounces whole wheat fusilli or penne pasta
- 3 cups broth
- 24 ounces enchilada sauce
- 2 cans black olives, pitted
- 4 pounds ground turkey or beef
- 4 tablespoons taco seasoning
- 4 cups shredded cheese
- 1 cup sour cream
- 1 cup cooked or canned black beans
- ½ cup corn kernels
- Fresh cilantro to garnish
- Salad, to serve (optional)

Directions:

1. Select the 'Sauté' button. Add meat and taco seasoning and cook until brown.
2. Add broth and enchilada sauce and mix well. Add pasta and stir.
3. Close the lid and lock it by setting the valve to the sealed position. Select the 'Manual' button and set the timer for 4 minutes.
4. When the timer goes off, quickly release the remaining pressure.
5. Add sour cream, black beans, and corn and mix well.
6. Transfer into a serving bowl.
7. Sprinkle cheese and olives on top, garnish with cilantro, and serve with salad of your choice.

CHAPTER 8:
MEDITERRANEAN DIET MEAT RECIPES

SLOPPY JOES

Preparation time: 15 minutes

Cooking time: 20 minutes

Number of servings: 4

Ingredients:

- ½ tablespoon avocado oil
- 1 medium onion, finely chopped (about ½ cup)
- Salt to taste
- 3 cloves garlic, minced
- 1/8 cup water
- ½ teaspoon dry mustard
- ½ tablespoon tomato paste
- Red chili flakes to taste
- 4 hamburger buns, split

- ¾ pound ground lean beef
- ½ cup finely diced red bell pepper
- Pepper to taste
- 2 tablespoons apple cider vinegar
- 1 ½ tablespoon brown sugar
- 2 teaspoons Worcestershire sauce
- 2 teaspoons chili powder or to taste
- ¾ cup canned, crushed and strained tomatoes
- 2 tablespoons butter or more if required

Directions:

1. Press the 'Sauté' button. Add oil and allow it to heat. Add the onion, beef, bell pepper, pepper, and salt and cook until the meat is no longer pink.
2. Discard cooked fat from the pot.
3. Stir in garlic and cook for a few seconds until fragrant.
4. Stir in vinegar, brown sugar, Worcestershire sauce, chili powder, mustard, tomato paste, tomatoes, water, and red pepper flakes. Press the 'Cancel' button.
5. Close the lid and lock it by setting the valve to the sealed position. Select the 'Manual' button and set the timer for 5 minutes.

6. When the timer goes off, allow the pressure to release naturally for 10 minutes, after which quickly release the remaining pressure.

7. Toast the buns to the desired doneness. Spread butter on the cut part of the buns.

8. Serve sloppy joes on the buns.

BEEF STUFFED PEPPERS

Preparation time: 15 minutes

Cooking time: 35 minutes

Number of servings: 8

Ingredients:

- 2 tablespoons olive oil
- 2 medium onions, diced
- 2 cans (6 ounces each) tomato paste
- 8 green bell peppers, slice off the top part near the stems, deseeded
- 2 pounds ground lean beef
- Water, as required
- 2 packages (1.25 ounces each) taco seasoning

Directions:

1. Press the 'Sauté' button. Add oil and allow it to heat. Add the onion and beef and cook until the meat is no longer pink.
2. Discard cooked fat from the pot.

3. Stir in tomato paste, 1 ½ cups water, and taco seasoning. Press the 'Cancel' button.

4. Stuff this mixture into the bell peppers.

5. Wipe the pot clean and add 1 ½ cups of water into the pot. Place a trivet in it and the bell peppers over the trivet.

6. Close the lid and lock it by setting the valve to the sealed position. Select the 'Manual' button and set the timer for 8 minutes.

7. When the timer goes off, allow the pressure to release naturally for 5 minutes, after which release the remaining pressure.

8. Serve hot.

SHEPHERD'S PIE WITH POTATOES AND YAMS

Preparation time: 20 minutes

Cooking time: 45 minutes

Number of servings: 5

Ingredients:

For topping:

- ½ cup chicken broth
- 1 medium russet potato, peeled, chopped
- ¼ cup milk
- 1 medium yam, peeled, chopped
- ½ teaspoon Himalayan pink salt
- 1 ½ tablespoons butter

For meat filling:

- ½ tablespoon olive oil
- 1 clove garlic, peeled, smashed
- Salt to taste
- ½ cup frozen corn kernels

- 1 cup diced broccoli
- ½ stalk celery, chopped
- Water, as required
- 1 small onion, chopped
- ¾ pound ground beef
- 3 mushrooms, sliced
- ½ cup frozen peas
- ½ cup chopped carrot
- ½ package (from a 0.87-ounce package) low-sodium gravy mix powder
- ¼ cup shredded cheddar cheese
- Pepper to taste

Directions:

1. Add broth into the instant pot. Keep a steamer rack in the pot. Place the potato and yam on top of it. Season with salt.

2. Close the lid and lock it by setting the valve to the sealed position. Select the 'Manual' button and set the timer for 8 minutes.

3. When the timer goes off, allow the pressure to release naturally for 5 minutes, after which release the remaining pressure.

4. Take out the yam and potato. Remove the rack as well. Pour the broth into a cup and set aside.

5. Add yam, potato, butter, and milk into the pot and mash until smooth with a potato masher. Transfer into a bowl. Set it aside to top later.

6. Clean the pot. Press the 'Sauté' button. Let the pot heat. Add oil. Once the oil is hot enough, add the onion and garlic and cook until the onion turns translucent.

7. Stir in the beef. Add salt and pepper to taste. Sauté for about 3 minutes.

8. Stir in the mushrooms and cook until tender.

9. Add vegetables into the pot and mix well. Add the retained broth. Press the 'Cancel' button.

10. Close the lid and lock it by setting the valve to the sealed position. Select the 'Manual' button and set the timer for 3 minutes.

11. When the timer goes off, allow the pressure to release naturally for 5 minutes, after which release the remaining pressure.

12. Discard any extra liquid from the pot.

13. Select the 'Sauté' button.

14. Whisk gravy mix with a little water and pour into the pot. Mix well. Simmer until thick. Press the 'Cancel' button.

15. Spoon the mixture into a baking dish. Spread the mashed potato and yam mixture over the filling.

16. Scatter cheddar cheese on top.

17. Preheat the oven to 350°F and bake for about 10 minutes.

18. Set the oven to broil mode and broil for a few minutes until brown on top.

19. Remove the baking dish from the oven. Set it on the counter to cool for a few minutes.

20. Serve.

BEEF FAJITAS

Preparation time: 15 minutes

Cooking time: 20 minutes

Number of servings: 4

Ingredients:

- ¾ pound beef top sirloin steak, cut into thin strips
- ¼ teaspoon seasoned salt or to taste
- Crushed red pepper flakes to taste
- 1 tablespoon lemon juice
- ¼ cup water
- ½ large onion, thinly sliced
- ½ large sweet red pepper, thinly sliced
- ¾ teaspoon ground cumin
- ¼ teaspoon chili powder
- 1 tablespoon olive oil
- 2 small cloves garlic, minced
- 4 whole wheat tortillas, warmed

Optional toppings:

- Avocado slices
- ½ cup shredded cheddar cheese
- 1 jalapeño pepper, sliced
- 1 tomato, chopped

Directions:

1. Place steak in a bowl. Sprinkle seasoned salt, cumin, red pepper flakes and chili powder over it and toss well.

2. Press the 'Sauté' button. Let the pot heat. Add oil. Once the oil is hot enough, add the beef and cook until brown. Remove the beef and set it aside.

3. Pour water into the pot. Add lemon juice and garlic and mix well. Scrape the base of the pot to remove any remaining stuck pieces. Select the 'Cancel' button.

4. Add beef into the pot.

5. Close the lid and lock it by setting the valve to the sealed position. Select the 'Meat/Stew' button and set the timer for 20 minutes.

6. When the timer goes off, allow the pressure to release naturally for 10 minutes, after which release the remaining pressure.

7. Take out only the meat and set it aside.

8. Add the onions into the cooking pot along with red pepper.

9. Close the lid and lock it by setting the valve to the sealed position. Select the 'Manual' button and set the timer for 5 minutes.

10. When the timer goes off, release the remaining pressure.

11. Place tortillas on individual serving plates. Divide the meat among the tortillas. Divide the onion and red pepper among the tortillas. Place any of the optional toppings and serve.

MEDITERRANEAN INSTANT POT SHREDDED BEEF

Preparation time: 5 minutes

Cooking time: 20 minutes

Number of servings: 4

Ingredients:

- 1 pound beef chuck roast
- ½ cup chopped white onion
- ½ yellow bell pepper, chopped
- 1 tablespoon red wine vinegar
- ½ tablespoon Italian seasoning blend
- ½ teaspoon salt
- 1 small carrot, chopped
- ½ can (from a 14.5 ounce can) fire roasted tomatoes
- ½ tablespoon minced garlic
- 1 teaspoon red pepper flakes

Directions:

1. Place meat in the cooking pot in the instant pot. Place the rest of the ingredients over the meat.

2. Close the lid and lock it by setting the valve to the sealed position. Select the 'Meat/Stew' button and set the timer for 20 minutes.

3. When the timer goes off, allow the pressure to release naturally for 10 minutes, after which release the remaining pressure.

4. Uncover and let it sit for 10 minutes.

5. Remove the meat from the pot and place it on the cutting board.

6. Shred the meat with a fork. Add the shredded meat into the pot. Mix well and serve.

MEDITERRANEAN PORK TENDERLOIN WITH COUSCOUS

Preparation time: 10 minutes

Cooking time: 40 minutes

Number of servings: 8

Ingredients:

- 2 cups chicken broth
- 4 pork tenderloins (12 ounces each), trimmed
- Salt to taste
- 8 cloves garlic, minced, divided
- Freshly ground pepper to taste
- ½ tablespoons Italian seasoning
- 2 cups couscous
- 1 cup sliced almonds, toasted
- 1 cup minced fresh parsley
- 1 cup raisins
- 1 cup extra-virgin olive oil
- ¼ cup red wine vinegar

Directions:

1. Add 6 cloves minced garlic and broth into the cooking pot in the instant pot.
2. Dry the meat by patting with paper towels. Add Italian seasoning, salt, and pepper into a bowl and stir.
3. Rub this mixture over the meat and place it in the instant pot.
4. Close the lid and lock it by setting the valve to the sealed position. Select the 'Meat/Stew' button and set the timer for 30 minutes.
5. When the timer goes off, allow the pressure to release naturally.
6. Remove the meat and place it on your cutting board. Cover it loosely with foil.
7. Retain 2 cups of liquid in the pot and discard the rest.
8. Add couscous and raisins into the pot. Stir well.
9. Close the lid and lock it by setting the valve to the sealed position. Select the 'Manual' button and set the timer for 10 minutes.
10. When the timer goes off, quickly release the excess pressure.
11. Uncover and loosen the couscous using a fork.
12. Add almonds and stir.

13. To make parsley vinaigrette: Add remaining garlic, vinegar, parsley, oil, salt and pepper into a bowl and whisk it well.

14. Once the meat has cooled enough to handle, cut into slices.

15. Divide couscous onto plates. Place meat on top. Drizzle parsley vinaigrette on top and serve.

GREEN BEANS WITH PORK AND POTATOES

Preparation time: 15 minutes

Cooking time: 17 minutes

Number of servings: 4

Ingredients:

- ½ pound lean pork, cut into bite-size pieces
- ¼ cup extra-virgin olive oil
- 1 stalk celery, thinly sliced
- ½ pound green beans, trimmed
- Salt to taste
- ½ large onion, chopped
- 1 carrot, thinly sliced
- 2 fresh tomatoes, grated
- 1 potato quartered
- Pepper to taste

Directions:

1. Press the 'Sauté' button. Let the pot heat. Add oil and allow it to heat. Add the pork and cook for 3 – 4 minutes stirring occasionally.

2. Add the remaining ingredients and mix well. Press the 'Cancel' button.

3. Close the lid and lock it by setting the valve to the sealed position. Select the 'Manual' button and set the timer for 17 minutes.

4. When the timer goes off, allow the pressure to release naturally.

5. Stir and serve. Make sure there is a potato piece in each serving.

MEDITERRANEAN LEG OF LAMB ROAST

Preparation time: 15 minutes

Cooking time: 50 – 55 minutes

Number of servings: 4 – 6

Ingredients:

For roast:

- 2 ½ - 3 pounds leg of lamb, bone-in or boneless
- 1 ¼ - 1 ½ pound potatoes, peeled, cut into bite-size cubes

- 1 cup broth
- 1 tablespoon extra-virgin olive oil
- ½ teaspoon salt
- ¼ teaspoon pepper or to taste
- ½ teaspoon dried sage
- ½ teaspoon dried marjoram
- 2 cloves garlic, minced
- ½ teaspoon dried thyme
- ½ teaspoon ground ginger
- 2 small bay leaves, crushed
- 1-1 ½ tablespoons cornstarch or arrowroot powder mixed with 3 – 4 tablespoons water (optional)

Directions:

1. Press the 'Sauté' button. Let the pot heat. Add oil and allow it to heat. Add lamb and turn it around in the pot so that it is coated with oil.
2. Cook for 2 - 3 minutes on each side.
3. Add salt, spices, and herbs and mix well. Press the 'Cancel' button.

4. Close the lid and lock it by setting the valve to the sealed position. Select the 'Manual' button and set the timer for 45 minutes.

5. When the timer goes off, quickly release the excess pressure.

6. Add potatoes and stir.

7. Close the lid and lock it by setting the valve to the sealed position. Select the 'Manual' button and set the timer for 10 minutes.

8. When the timer goes off, allow the pressure to release naturally for 5 minutes and then release extra pressure.

9. Fish out the potatoes and meat and set aside in a serving bowl.

10. Add cornstarch mixture into the pot.

11. Press the 'Sauté' button and simmer for a few minutes until thick, stirring constantly.

12. Press the 'Cancel' button.

13. Pour gravy over lamb and potatoes.

14. Serve.

MEDITERRANEAN LAMB SHANKS

Preparation time: 40 minutes

Cooking time: 90 minutes

Number of servings: 6 – 8

Ingredients:

For marinade:

- ½ cup olive oil
- 4 tablespoons brown sugar
- 1 teaspoon ground cumin
- 6 cloves garlic, minced
- 2 tablespoons dried oregano
- 2 tablespoons kosher salt
- 2 tablespoons smoked paprika
- 2 sticks cinnamon (2 inches each)

For lamb:

- 3 – 4 pounds skinless lamb shanks
- 2 onions, chopped

- 4 bay leaves
- 8 cups warm beef broth
- ½ cup chopped Italian parsley, to garnish (optional)
- ½ cup olive oil
- 6 carrots, chopped
- 4 cups red wine
- 6 tablespoons cornstarch mixed with 6 tablespoons water

Directions:

1. Add all the ingredients for marinade into a large bowl and mix well.
2. Place the lamb shanks in it and turn them around so that they are well coated. Let them rest for about 30 – 40 minutes.
3. Press the 'Sauté' button. Let the pot heat. Add oil and allow it to heat. Add half the lamb (no marinade) and turn it around in the pot so that it is coated with oil.
4. Cook for 2 - 3 minutes on each side or until brown. Remove the meat and place it in a bowl.
5. Add remaining lamb (but retain marinade) and cook until lamb is brown all over. If your pot is small, cook in batches. Place it in the bowl along with the browned lamb. Tent the bowl with foil.

6. Add carrots, onion, bay leaf and retained marinade into the instant pot and cook until the onions turn translucent.

7. Pour in the wine and scrape the base of the pot to dislodge any brown bits that may be stuck.

8. Add broth and lamb and stir. Press the 'Cancel' button.

9. Close the lid and lock it by setting the valve to the sealed position. Select the 'Meat/Stew' button and set the timer for 30 minutes.

10. When the timer goes off, allow the pressure to release naturally for 5 minutes and then release the extra pressure.

11. Take out the meat from the pot and place in a bowl. Tent with foil loosely.

12. Pour the liquid from the pot into a strainer placed over a bowl and discard the solids.

13. Pour the strained liquid back into the pot.

14. Add cornstarch mixture into the pot.

15. Press the 'Sauté' button and simmer until the sauce is thick. Stir constantly. Press the 'Cancel' button.

16. Pour gravy on top. Sprinkle parsley on top and serve with rice or noodles.

CHAPTER 9:
MEDITERRANEAN SEAFOOD RECIPES

INSTANT POT FROZEN SALMON

Preparation time: 5 minutes

Cooking time: 3 minutes

Number of servings: 4

Ingredients:

- 1 ½ cups water
- Salt to taste
- Pepper to taste
- ½ cup lemon juice
- 4 frozen salmon fillets
- 4 tablespoons balsamic vinegar
- 4 tablespoons honey

Directions:

1. Add water and lemon juice into the cooking pot in the instant pot. Spray a steamer rack with cooking spray and place it in the instant pot.

2. Combine honey and vinegar in a bowl.

3. Lay the fillets on the rack, with the skin side touching the rack. Brush some of the honey mixture on top.

4. Close the lid and lock it by setting the valve to the sealed position. Select the 'Manual' button and set the timer for 3 – 4 minutes, depending on the size of the fillets.

5. When the timer goes off, quickly release the excess pressure.

6. Sprinkle salt and pepper over the salmon. Brush on some more honey mixture. Cover and Select the 'Keep Warm' until use.

SALMON FILLETS AND VEGETABLES

Preparation time: 10 minutes

Cooking time: 3 – 4 minutes

Number of servings: 4

Ingredients:

- 4 salmon fillets (5 ounces each)
- Salt to taste
- 4 tablespoons honey
- Pepper to taste
- 2 teaspoons sesame seeds (optional)
- 2 packages (12 ounces each) frozen Asian stir fry vegetable blend, do not thaw
- 4 tablespoons soy sauce
- 4 tablespoons lemon juice

To serve:

- Hot cooked brown rice

Directions:

1. Place frozen vegetables in the cooking pot in the instant pot.
2. Sprinkle salt and pepper over the salmon and place over thc vegetables.
3. Combine honey, soy sauce, and lemon juice in a bowl and pour over the salmon.
4. Close the lid and lock it by setting the valve to the sealed position. Select the 'Manual' button and set the timer for 4 minutes.
5. When the timer goes off, quickly release the excess pressure.
6. Sprinkle sesame seeds over the salmon. Cover and select the 'Keep Warm' function until use.
7. Serve fillets over hot cooked brown rice. Spoon sauce mixture over the rice and fillets and serve.

MEDITERRANEAN PASTA WITH TUNA AND TOMATOES

Preparation time: 10 minutes

Cooking time: About 25 minutes

Number of servings: 2

Ingredients:

- 4 ounces dry, fusilli pasta (multigrain or whole wheat)
- 1 cup water
- ½ can (from a 14 ounce can) diced tomatoes with Italian seasonings, with its liquid
- 1/8 cup pitted, brine cured black olives, quartered
- ½ can (from a 6 ounce can) water packed tuna, do not drain
- 1 teaspoon minced fresh oregano, to garnish
- ½ tablespoon extra-virgin olive oil
- ¼ cup fresh Italian parsley, chopped
- 1/3 cup brine cured capers
- Salt to taste

- ½ tablespoon of a lemon
- Pepper to taste
- 1 teaspoon grated lemon zest

Directions:

1. Add pasta and water into the cooking pot in the instant pot. Stir well.
2. Close the lid and lock it by setting the valve to the sealed position. Select the 'Manual' button and set the timer for 4 minutes.
3. When the timer goes off, quickly release the excess pressure.
4. Transfer into a bowl.
5. Wipe the pot clean.
6. Select the 'Sauté' button. Add oil and allow it to heat. Add tomatoes, olives, and capers and cook for 2 - 3 minutes. Stir occasionally.
7. Add parsley, lemon juice, and lemon zest and mix well.
8. Add tuna and pasta, stir. Sprinkle some water if it seems too dry. Simmer for a few minutes. Press the 'Cancel' button.
9. Garnish with oregano and serve.

ITALIAN FISH

Preparation time: 10 minutes

Cooking time: 20 minutes

Number of servings: 2

Ingredients:

- 2 frozen white fish fillets
- 3 – 4 tablespoons water
- 6 cherry tomatoes
- 1 tablespoon marinated baby capers
- 1 tablespoon olive oil
- Chili flakes to taste
- 6 – 7 black olives, pitted, sliced
- 3 tablespoons sliced roasted red peppers
- Salt to taste
- Chopped parsley or basil, to garnish (optional)

Directions:

1. Pour water into the cooking pot in the instant pot. Place fish in the pot, over the water.

2. Place the rest of the ingredients over the fish.

3. Close the lid and lock it by setting the valve to the sealed position. Select the 'Manual' button and set the timer for 4 minutes.

4. When the timer goes off, allow the pressure to release naturally for 7 – 8 minutes, after which quickly release the excess pressure.

5. Serve hot.

LEMON PEPPER SALMON

Preparation time: 5 minutes

Cooking time: 5 – 6 minutes

Number of servings: 6

Ingredients:

- 2 pounds salmon fillets, with skin
- Salt to taste
- 1 lemon, thinly sliced
- 2 red bell peppers, cut into thin strips

- A handful sprigs of dill, parsley, tarragon, or basil or a mixture of these
- 6 teaspoons olive oil or ghee, divided
- 1 teaspoon pepper or to taste
- 2 zucchinis, trimmed, cut into matchsticks
- 2 carrots, peeled, cut into matchsticks

Directions:

1. Pour water into the cooking pot of the instant pot. Add herbs and place a steamer rack in such a way that it sits above the water.
2. Lay the salmon on the rack with the skin side touching the top of the rack.
3. Trickle oil over the salmon. Sprinkle salt and pepper over the salmon. Be generous with the pepper. Place lemon slices on top of the salmon. The salmon should be covered with lemon slices so use as many as needed.
4. Close the lid and lock it by setting the valve to the sealed position. Select the 'Steam' button and set the timer for 3 to 4 minutes, depending on the thickness of the fillets. For a 1 inch fillet, set it for 3 minutes. For fillets thicker than 1 inch, set it for 4 minutes.

5. When the timer goes off, release the excess pressure. Discard the herb sprigs.

6. Add all the vegetables into the pot.

7. Select the 'Sauté' button. Simmer for a couple of minutes.

8. Place salmon on individual serving plates. Top with vegetables. Drizzle some of the cooked liquid on the vegetables and serve.

PAELLA WITH CAULIFLOWER RICE

Preparation time: 20 minutes

Cooking time: 20 minutes

Number of servings: 3

Ingredients:

- 6 ounces chicken breast, cut into 1 inch pieces
- 1 teaspoon Spanish smoked paprika
- 1 medium head cauliflower, grated to rice like texture
- 1 sausage link, cut into ½ inch slices
- 1 medium onion, diced
- ½ cup chicken stock
- Handful of fresh parsley, chopped to garnish
- 1 ½ tablespoons olive oil
- ½ teaspoon dried oregano
- A pinch of saffron threads
- 1 bay leaf
- ½ teaspoon turmeric powder
- ½ pound whole shrimp, peeled, deveined

- 2 cloves garlic, minced
- 3 sprigs thyme
- ½ cup frozen green peas, thawed
- Salt to taste
- Lemon wedges for garnishing

Directions:

1. Place chicken in a bowl. Drizzle oil over it. Sprinkle oregano and paprika over it and rub them well into the chicken.

2. Press the 'Sauté' button. Add a tablespoon of olive oil to the pot. Add sausage and cook until brown all over. Remove sausage and set aside on a plate.

3. Add more oil if needed. Then add chicken to the instant pot and cook until done and no longer pink inside, approximately 8 minutes. Remove and transfer to a plate.

4. Add the onion and saffron and sauté for a minute. Add garlic and stir for 30 – 40 seconds or until aromatic.

5. Add cauliflower rice, turmeric powder, and bay leaf and mix well. Press the 'Cancel' button. Add the chicken stock, sausage, and chicken and stir.

6. Place thyme sprigs, peas, and shrimp. Do not stir.

7. Close the lid and lock it by setting the valve to the sealed position. Select the 'Manual' button and set the timer for 1 minute.

8. When the timer goes off, quickly release the excess pressure.

9. Discard thyme and take out the shrimp.

10. Transfer the contents of the pot into a strainer placed over a bowl. Discard the strained liquid.

11. Transfer the paella into a serving bowl. Place shrimp on top.

12. Garnish with parsley.

13. Serve hot with lemon wedges.

SHRIMP FRA DIAVOLO PASTA

Preparation time: 5 minutes

Cooking time: 10 minutes

Number of servings: 3

Ingredients:

- ½ tablespoon olive oil
- ½ small fennel bulb, cored, thinly sliced
- Crushed red pepper to taste
- 1 1/3 cups water
- ½ pound dried whole wheat pasta of your choice
- 1 ½ tablespoons light cream
- Salt to taste
- Pepper to taste
- 1 medium onion, chopped
- 3 cloves garlic, peeled, minced
- 1 can (14 ounces) crushed tomatoes
- 3 tablespoons cognac or brandy
- ½ pound raw jumbo shrimp, peeled, deveined

- 1 tablespoon chopped parsley

Directions:

1. Select the 'Sauté' button. Let the pot heat. Add oil and allow it to heat. Add the onion, garlic, fennel, and crushed pepper. Cook for a couple of minutes.

2. Stir in pasta, tomatoes, cognac, water, and salt. Press the 'Cancel' button.

3. Close the lid and lock it by setting the valve to the sealed position. Select the 'Manual' button and set the timer for 4 minutes.

4. When the timer goes off, quickly release the excess pressure.

5. Uncover and add shrimp, parsley, and cream and stir. Cook until the shrimp turns pink.

6. Add salt and pepper to taste.

7. Cool for a few minutes and serve.

SALMON WITH CHILI LIME SAUCE

Preparation time: 10 minutes

Cooking time: 3 – 4 minutes

Number of servings: 4

Ingredients:

For salmon:

- 1 ½ cups water
- Salt to taste
- Pepper to taste
- 4 frozen salmon fillets (5 – 7 ounces each)

For chili lime sauce:

- 4 cloves garlic, minced
- 2 tablespoons fresh lime juice
- 4 teaspoons hot water
- 1 teaspoon ground cumin
- 2 tablespoons sriracha sauce
- 2 tablespoons chopped cilantro

- 1 teaspoon smoked paprika

Directions:

1. In a bowl, add all the ingredients for the sauce and whisk them until thoroughly mixed. Cover and set aside so that the flavors blend together.
2. Add water into the instant pot. Spray a steamer rack with cooking spray and place it in the instant pot.
3. Lay the fillets on the rack, with the skin side touching the rack.
4. Close the lid and lock it by setting the valve to the sealed position. Select the 'Manual' button and set the timer for 3 – 4 minutes, depending on the size of the fillets.
5. When the timer goes off, quickly release the excess pressure.
6. Sprinkle salt and pepper over the salmon. Cover and Select the 'Keep Warm' until use.
7. Place salmon on individual serving plates. Drizzle sauce on top of the salmon and serve right away.

QUICK AND EASY SHRIMP CURRY

Preparation time: 5 minutes

Cooking time: 15 minutes

Number of servings: 8

Ingredients:

- 3 pounds jumbo or extra-large shrimp, tail on, peeled, deveined
- 2 cans coconut milk, chilled for 5 – 6 hours
- 2 medium yellow onions, finely sliced
- 2 green cardamom pods
- Salt to taste
- ½ teaspoon turmeric powder
- 4 teaspoons minced garlic
- 4 teaspoons minced ginger
- 1 cup tomato puree
- 2 tablespoons oil
- 2 sticks cinnamon (2 inches each)
- 12 whole cloves

- 2 teaspoons Kashmiri chili powder
- 1 cup tomato puree
- A handful fresh cilantro, chopped, to garnish

Directions:

1. Open the cans of coconut milk. Skim off the coconut cream on top and set aside the coconut cream as well as the coconut water.

2. Select the 'Sauté' button. Add oil. Once the oil is hot enough, add the whole spices and onion and cook until the onion turns translucent.

3. Stir in salt and remaining spices. Select the 'Cancel' button.

4. Add tomato puree, about ½ cup of the retained coconut water, tomato puree, and shrimp and mix well.

5. Close the lid and lock it by setting the valve to the sealed position. Select the 'Manual' button and set the timer for 2 minutes.

6. When the timer goes off, quickly release the excess pressure.

7. Add coconut cream and stir. Sprinkle cilantro on top.

8. Serve hot.

ONE POT SHRIMP AND VEGGIES

Preparation time: 10 minutes

Cooking time: 8 – 10 minutes

Number of servings: 5 – 6

Ingredients:

- 2 pounds shrimp, peeled, deveined
- 4 cups cherry tomatoes, halved or quartered depending on the size
- 6 cloves garlic, minced
- Olive oil, as required
- Lemon wedges to serve
- Pepper to taste
- 2 medium white onions, chopped into ½ inch pieces
- 2 medium green bell peppers, chopped into ½ inch pieces
- 6 – 8 stalks celery, chopped into ½ inch pieces
- Salt to taste

Directions:

1. Select the 'Sauté' button. Add a little olive oil or spray with olive oil spray.

2. When the pot is heated, add the onion and cook for a couple of minutes.

3. Stir in the celery and bell peppers and cook until slightly tender.

4. Stir in cherry tomatoes and garlic and cook for a minute.

5. Add shrimp and sprinkle a little water.

6. Select the 'Cancel' button.

7. Close the lid and lock it by setting the valve to the sealed position. Select the 'Manual' button and set the timer for 1 minute.

8. When the timer goes off, release excess pressure.

9. Add salt and pepper to taste.

10. Serve hot.

SHRIMP AND TOMATOES WITH WARM SPICES

Preparation time: 10 minutes

Cooking time: 50 minutes

Number of servings: 8

Ingredients:

- 2 pounds large shrimp, peeled, deveined
- 10 cloves garlic, peeled, minced, divided
- 1 teaspoon salt divided
- 2 bell peppers of any color, deseeded, chopped
- 2 tablespoons ras el hanout
- 2 cans (28 ounces each) whole, peeled tomatoes, drained but retain the juice, coarsely chopped
- ¼ cup chopped fresh parsley
- 4 tablespoons extra-virgin olive oil, divided + extra to drizzle
- 2 teaspoons grated lemon zest
- Pepper to taste
- 2 small onions, chopped

- 1 teaspoon ground ginger
- ½ cup pitted, brine-cured green or black olives, coarsely chopped
- 4 scallions, thinly sliced

Directions:

1. Place shrimp in a bowl. Add half of each – garlic, oil, and salt. Also add lemon zest and pepper. Toss well.
2. Cover and chill until use.
3. Select the 'Sauté' button. Add 2 tablespoons of oil and allow it to heat. add the onion, bell pepper, and ½ teaspoon salt and mix well. Cook until the onions turn translucent.
4. Add the remaining garlic, ginger, and ras el hanout and mix well. Cook for a few seconds until aromatic.
5. Add tomatoes and retained juice. Mix well and press the 'Cancel' button.
6. Close the lid and lock it by setting the valve to the sealed position. Select the 'Manual' button and set the timer for 15 minutes.
7. When the timer goes off, release excess pressure.
8. Add shrimp and stir. Close the lid once again and let it rest for about 7 – 8 minutes.

9. Add olives, salt, pepper, and parsley and mix well.
10. Garnish with scallions. Trickle some oil on top and serve.

TOMATO AND SHRIMP ORZO

Preparation time: 15 minutes

Cooking time: 15 minutes

Number of servings: 8

Ingredients:

- 2 tablespoons olive oil
- 4 cloves garlic, minced
- 4 tablespoons chopped fresh parsley
- 2 ½ pounds medium shrimp, peeled, deveined
- Freshly ground pepper to taste
- 2 ½ cups chicken stock
- 2 medium onions, diced
- 4 cans (14.5 ounces each) diced tomatoes with their juices
- ¼ cup chopped fresh dill
- Salt to taste
- 1 1/3 cups feta cheese, crumbled
- 1 ½ cups orzo

Directions:

1. Select the 'Sauté' button. Let the pot heat. Add 2 tablespoons of oil and allow it to heat. Once the oil is hot enough, add the onion and garlic and cook until the onions turn brown.
2. Sprinkle some water and remove browned bits by scraping the base of the pot.
3. Pour stock into the pot. Add tomatoes and let the stock begin boiling. Press the 'Cancel' button.
4. Stir in orzo and herbs. Place shrimp in the pot. Sprinkle salt and pepper over the shrimp.
5. Scatter feta cheese.
6. Close the lid and lock it by setting the valve to the sealed position. Select the 'Manual' button and set the timer for 3 minutes.
7. When the timer goes off, release the excess pressure.
8. Stir and serve.

CHAPTER 10: MEDITERRANEAN DIET VEGETARIAN RECIPES

MAKHANI DAAL (BUTTERY LENTILS)

Preparation time: 10 minutes + soaking time

Cooking time: 25 minutes

Number of servings: 3 – 4

Ingredients:

- ½ cup dried black lentils, rinsed, soaked in water overnight
- A handful dried kidney beans, rinsed, soaked in water overnight
- A handful dried split chickpeas, rinsed, soaked in water overnight
- 1 teaspoon olive oil or ghee
- ½ onion, finely chopped
- 1 clove garlic, peeled, minced

- 1 inch fresh ginger, peeled, minced
- ½ teaspoon cumin seeds
- 1 teaspoon ground coriander
- ¼ teaspoon chili powder
- ½ teaspoon garam masala
- 1 tomato, finely chopped
- ¼ teaspoon red chili powder
- Salt to taste
- 1 tablespoon yogurt
- 2 teaspoons butter
- Salt to taste
- Hot cooked rice, to serve (optional)

Directions:

1. Drain the water from the lentils, kidney beans, and chickpeas and place in the instant pot.
2. Pour enough water to cover at least 2 inches above the lentils and beans.
3. Close the lid and lock it by setting the valve to the sealed position. Select the 'Beans/Chili' button and set the timer for 25 minutes.

4. When the timer goes off, allow the pressure to release naturally.

5. Heat a skillet, pour oil in it, when it is hot enough, add cumin seeds. When they crackle, add the onion and cook until it becomes translucent.

6. Stir in ginger and garlic and cook for about a minute, until fragrant. Stir in tomatoes and cook until soft.

7. Add spices and salt and mix well. Pour into the instant pot and stir.

8. Select the 'Sauté' button and simmer for a few minutes until the onion mixture is well blended with the lentil mixture.

9. Add butter and yogurt and stir.

10. Garnish with cilantro and serve over hot cooked rice.

TWO BEAN BURRITOS

Preparation time: 10 minutes

Cooking time: 2 – 3 hours

Number of servings: 4

Ingredients:

- ½ can (from a 15 ounce can) diced tomatoes with green chilies
- ½ can (from a 15 ounce can) black beans, rinsed, drained
- ½ can (from a 15 ounce can) pinto beans, rinsed, drained
- ½ can (from a 15 ounce can) corn kernels, drained
- 4 fat-free flour tortillas (8 inches each), warmed according to the instructions on the package
- 1 ½ tablespoons Mexican or taco seasoning or to taste
- ¼ cup fat free sour cream

Optional toppings:

- Salsa
- Low- fat cheese
- Any other toppings of your choice

Directions:

1. Discard about ¼ cup of liquid from the diced tomatoes and add the rest of the tomatoes with the remaining liquid, pinto beans, black beans, seasoning, and corn into the instant pot and stir.

2. Close the lid and lock it by setting the valve to the sealed position. Select the 'Slow' button and set the timer for 2-3 hours.

3. When the timer goes off, uncover and mash the mixture with a potato masher until coarse in texture.

4. Warm the tortillas following the instructions on the package. Place the tortillas on your countertop. Place about ½ cup bean mixture on each tortilla.

5. Drizzle sour cream over the beans. Top with salsa, cheese and any other toppings of your choice.

6. Fold like a burrito.

7. Serve immediately.

FARRO WITH TOMATOES

Preparation time: 10 minutes

Cooking time: 10 minutes

Number of servings: 4

Ingredients:

- 2 cups semi-pearled farro, rinsed, soaked in water for about 10 minutes
- 4 cups water
- 1 large onion, chopped
- 18 ounces grape or cherry tomatoes
- ½ teaspoon red pepper flakes or more to taste
- A handful fresh basil leaves, thinly sliced
- 4 cloves garlic, peeled, thinly sliced
- 2 ½ teaspoons kosher salt or coarse sea salt, or to taste
- Grated parmesan cheese to serve
- 2 tablespoons olive oil + extra to drizzle

Directions:

1. Drain and add farro into the cooking pot in the instant pot. Add oil, salt, and red pepper flakes into the pot and stir for 4 – 5 seconds.

2. Add water, onion, garlic, and tomato and stir.

3. Close the lid and lock it by setting the valve to the sealed position. Select the 'Manual' button and set the timer for 7 minutes.

4. When the timer goes off, allow the pressure to release naturally.

5. Transfer into a bowl. Garnish with parmesan and basil and serve.

BARLEY RISOTTO WITH TOMATOES AND MARINATED FETA

Preparation time: 15 minutes

Cooking time: 25 minutes

Number of servings: 8

Ingredients:

For risotto:

- 3 tablespoons butter
- 2 medium white onions, diced
- 8 cloves garlic, finely chopped
- 4 tablespoons olive oil
- 2 medium celery sticks, diced
- 3 cups uncooked pearl barley, rinsed
- 1 teaspoon chili flakes
- 1 teaspoon paprika
- 8 sprigs fresh thyme or 2 teaspoons dried thyme
- 2 cans (14.1 ounces each) tomatoes

- 6 cups vegetable stock
- 2 teaspoons salt or to taste
- 6 strips lemon rind
- 2 bay leaves
- 4 tablespoons tomato paste

For marinated feta:

- 2 tablespoons caraway or cumin seeds
- 18 – 20 ounces feta, cubed
- 1 cup olive oil
- A handful fresh oregano, chopped, to garnish

Directions:

1. Select the 'Sauté' button. Add butter and oil and allow it to melt.
2. Add the onion and celery and cook for about 3 minutes. Stir in garlic and cook for a couple of minutes.
3. Stir in bay leaves, barley, lemon rind, thyme, chili, and paprika and mix well. Select the 'Cancel' function.
4. Add the rest of the ingredients and mix well.

5. Close the lid and lock it by setting the valve to the sealed position. Select the 'Multigrain' button and set the timer for 20 minutes.

6. Meanwhile, make marinated feta in the following manner: Heat a pan over low flame and add oil and caraway seeds. Heat for 3 – 4 minutes. Turn off the heat and let it cool for 5 minutes.

7. Add feta and parsley into a bowl. Pour the oil over it and let it marinate.

8. When the timer goes off, allow the pressure to release naturally for 5 minutes, after which release the extra pressure.

9. Stir and serve into plates. Top with marinated feta and serve.

VEGETABLE LASAGNA

Preparation time: 15 minutes

Cooking time: 23 minutes

Number of servings: 4

Ingredients:

- ½ cup finely chopped zucchini
- 1 small onion, finely chopped
- ½ cup finely chopped mushrooms

- 1 cup chopped spinach or kale
- 1 bell pepper, finely chopped
- 1 small carrot, finely chopped
- 2 cloves garlic, finely chopped
- 13 ounces marinara sauce
- 4 – 5 whole wheat lasagna noodles, broken
- 1 small egg
- 7.5 ounces reduced fat ricotta cheese
- ½ cup shredded mozzarella cheese + extra to top
- 1 teaspoon dried basil or oregano
- 2 tablespoons chopped fresh parsley

Directions:

1. Spray the (heatproof and oven-safe) instant pot accessory pan that fits well in the instant pot with cooking spray. You can also use a springform pan.
2. Combine all the vegetables in a microwave safe bowl.
3. Microwave on High for 2 – 4 minutes. When they are cool enough to handle, squeeze excess moisture from the vegetables.
4. Add ricotta, egg, and basil in a bowl. Mix well.

5. Spread about 1/3 cup of tomato sauce on the bottom of the prepared pan.

6. Spread about 1/3 of the lasagna pieces over it.

7. Spread 1/3 of the vegetable mixture followed by 1/3 of mozzarella cheese. Spread 1/3 of the remaining sauce.

8. Repeat steps 6 – 7 twice.

9. Finally, spread a thin layer of sauce. Sprinkle some mozzarella on top.

10. Pour 1 ½ cups water into the cooking pot in the instant pot. Place a trivet in it and the lasagna pan over it.

11. Close the lid and lock it by setting the valve to the sealed position. Select the 'Manual' button and set the timer for 20 minutes.

12. When the timer goes off, allow the pressure to release naturally for 10 minutes, after which release the extra pressure.

13. Meanwhile, set the oven to broil mode. Preheat the oven.

14. Transfer the dish from the instant pot into the oven and broil for a few minutes until brown on top. This step is optional.

15. Sprinkle parsley over it. Slice and serve.

SPRING VEGETABLE BROWN RICE RISOTTO

Preparation time: 10 minutes

Cooking time: 35 minutes

Number of servings: 8

Ingredients:

- 2 teaspoons olive oil
- 1 leek, sliced, light green and white part only
- 2 cups snap peas
- 3 cups short grain brown rice, rinsed
- 6 ½ cups vegetable broth
- Freshly cracked pepper to taste
- 2 small shallots, minced
- 2 small bunches asparagus, discard hard ends, cut into 1 inch pieces
- 1 cup frozen green peas
- ½ cup dry white wine
- Salt to taste
- 1 ½ cups freshly grated parmesan cheese

Directions:

1. Select the 'Sauté' button. Add oil. Once the oil is hot enough, add leek, shallots, peas, and asparagus and stir. When the asparagus turns bright green in color, transfer the vegetables into a bowl.

2. Add wine and rice into the pot. Remove stuck particles from the base of the pot by scraping them.

3. Simmer until dry. Pour in broth. Select the 'Cancel' button.

4. Close the lid and lock it by setting the valve to the sealed position. Select the 'Multigrain' button. Set the timer for 35 minutes.

5. After the timer goes off, allow the pressure to release naturally for 10 – 12 minutes, after which release the extra pressure.

6. Add the sautéed vegetables and parmesan cheese and stir.

7. Select the 'Sauté' button and heat thoroughly.

8. Serve hot.

WHOLE WHEAT SPAGHETTI WITH MARINARA

Preparation time: 5 minutes

Cooking time: 5 minutes

Number of servings: 8

Ingredients:

- 16 ounces whole wheat spaghetti, break into 2 halves
- 4 cups water
- 5 cups marinara sauce
- Freshly grated parmesan cheese, as required

Directions:

1. Add water, spaghetti, and marinara sauce into the instant pot and stir.
2. Close the lid and lock it by setting the valve to the sealed position. Select the 'Manual' button and set the timer for 4 minutes.
3. When the timer goes off, release the extra pressure.
4. Add parmesan cheese and stir.
5. Serve hot.

MOROCCAN BAKED BEANS

Preparation time: 10 minutes

Cooking time: 30 minutes

Number of servings: 6 – 8

Ingredients:

- ½ pound dried white beans, rinsed
- ½ teaspoon ground cumin
- ½ teaspoon ground coriander
- 1 medium onion, chopped
- 1 small stick cinnamon (about 1 ½ inches)
- 2 carrots, peeled, chopped into chunks
- 1 tablespoon fresh lemon juice
- 2 tablespoons honey
- Pepper to taste
- 2 cups vegetable broth
- Salt to taste

Directions:

1. Place beans, onion, honey, carrots, broth, and spices into the cooking pot in the instant pot. Stir well.

2. Close the lid and lock it by setting the valve to the sealed position. Select the 'Beans/Chili' button and set the timer for 30 minutes.

3. When the timer goes off, allow the pressure to release naturally.

4. Add lemon juice, pepper, and salt and mix well. Discard the cinnamon stick.

5. Serve.

CHAPTER 11:
MEDITERRANEAN DIET VEGAN RECIPES

CHICKPEAS WITH SALSA VERDE

Preparation time: 15 minutes

Cooking time: 60 minutes

Number of servings: 8 – 10

Ingredients:

- 3 cups dried chickpeas, rinsed
- 2 vegetable stock cubes
- 8 cups water
- 4 roasted red peppers, thinly sliced
- 2 teaspoons tahini
- ½ cup vegan yogurt like soy or coconut
- A pinch ground cinnamon
- ½ teaspoon ground cumin

For salsa verde:

- 2 handfuls fresh basil
- 2 handfuls fresh parsley
- ¼ cup marinated capers
- 5 tablespoons lemon juice
- ½ cup olive oil
- 4 cloves garlic, peeled
- ½ teaspoon salt
- ½ teaspoon sugar (optional)

Directions:

1. Add chickpeas, water, and stock cubes into the cooking pot in the instant pot.
2. Close the lid and lock it by setting the valve to the sealed position. Select the 'Manual' button and set the timer for 45 minutes.
3. When the timer goes off, allow the pressure to release naturally.
4. Meanwhile, add salsa verde ingredients into a blender and blend until smooth. Pour into a bowl.
5. Combine yogurt and tahini in a bowl.

6. To assemble: Place chickpeas in a wide serving bowl. Spoon yogurt mixture in the center. Pour salsa Verde on the yogurt mixture.

7. Scatter roasted red pepper slices all over the chickpeas and serve.

BBQ LENTIL SLOPPY JOES

Preparation time: 15 minutes

Cooking time: 35 minutes

Number of servings: 8

Ingredients:

- 2 cups dried brown lentils, rinsed
- 2 medium carrots, diced
- 2 onions, diced
- 4 cloves garlic, sliced
- 5 cups water
- 2 tablespoons extra-virgin olive oil
- 2 cans (6 ounces each) tomato paste
- 1 tablespoon apple cider vinegar
- 4 tablespoons applesauce
- 3 teaspoons onion powder
- 3 teaspoons garlic powder
- 2 teaspoons dry mustard
- ¼ cup blackstrap molasses

- 2 teaspoons salt
- 1 teaspoon paprika
- 1 teaspoon pepper
- 1/8 teaspoon cayenne pepper
- ¼ teaspoon liquid smoke
- 8 whole wheat hamburger buns, to serve

<u>Optional toppings: Use any</u>

- Red cabbage, shredded
- Lettuce
- Avocado slices
- Onion slices
- Any other toppings of your choice

Directions:

1. Select the 'Sauté' button. Add oil. Once the oil is hot enough, add the onion and cook until it becomes translucent.
2. Stir in the carrots and cook until they begin to soften.
3. Stir in the garlic and cook for an additional few minutes.
4. Add the rest of the ingredients except buns and stir.

5. Close the lid and lock it by setting the valve to the sealed position. Select the 'Beans/Chili' button and set the timer for 20 minutes.

6. When the timer goes off, allow the pressure to release naturally for 5 minutes, after which release the extra pressure.

7. Split the buns and toast them to the desired doneness.

8. Serve lentils over the bottom half of the buns.

9. Place optional toppings if desired. Cover with the tops of the buns and serve.

PORTOBELLO POT ROAST

Preparation time: 10 minutes

Cooking time: 15 minutes

Number of servings: 10

Ingredients:

- 4 tablespoons olive oil
- 2 large onions, finely chopped
- 4 cloves garlic, peeled, finely chopped
- 10 potatoes, chopped into chunks
- 8 large carrots, cut into 3 inch pieces
- 10 large Portobello mushrooms, cut into ¾ inch thick slices
- 3 cups dry red wine
- 2 tablespoons soy sauce or tamari
- Salt to taste
- 2 tablespoons raw sugar
- 8 tablespoons arrowroot powder or cornstarch mixed with 4 – 5 tablespoons water

- 4 sprigs fresh thyme
- 8 fresh sage leaves
- 4 cups vegetable or mushroom broth
- 2 sprigs fresh rosemary
- Freshly cracked pepper to taste
- Fresh parsley, finely chopped to garnish (optional)

Directions:

1. Select the 'Sauté' button. Add 2 tablespoons of oil. Once the oil is hot enough, add mushrooms and cook until slightly brown. Remove into a bowl and set aside.
2. Add the remaining olive oil into the pot. Add the onions and cook until they caramelize.
3. Press the 'Cancel' button. Add garlic and stir constantly for about a minute.
4. Add potatoes, salt, pepper, carrots, soy sauce, sugar, wine, and broth into the pot and stir. Add more stock if required.
5. Scatter herbs on top.
6. Close the lid and lock it by setting the valve to the sealed position. Select the 'Manual' button and set the timer for 15 minutes.

7. When the timer goes off, release the pressure.

8. Select the 'Sauté' button. Add arrowroot mixture and stir constantly until thick.

9. Add mushrooms and stir well. Simmer for a few minutes.

10. Garnish with parsley and serve.

FASOLAKIA (GREEN BEANS AND POTATOES IN OLIVE OIL)

Preparation time: 10 minutes

Cooking time: 15 minutes

Number of servings: 8

Ingredients:

- 2 cans (15 ounces each) diced tomatoes
- 1 cup extra-virgin olive oil
- 2 bunches dill, chopped
- 1 bunch parsley, chopped
- 2 pounds green beans, trimmed
- 4 potatoes, quartered
- 2 cups water
- 2 large zucchinis, quartered
- 2 teaspoons dried oregano
- Pepper to taste
- 3 onions, thinly sliced
- Salt to taste

Directions:

1. Select the 'Sauté' button. Let the pot heat. Add water, tomatoes, and olive oil and stir.

2. Add the rest of the ingredients and mix very well.

3. Close the lid and lock it by setting the valve to the sealed position. Select the 'Manual' button and set the timer for 15 minutes.

4. When the timer goes off, quickly release the pressure.

5. Stir and serve.

LENTIL CURRY

Preparation time: 10 minutes

Cooking time: 15 minutes

Number of servings: 8

Ingredients:

- 3 cups green or brown lentils, rinsed
- 2 cups + 2 tablespoons water
- 6 tablespoons minced ginger
- 2 tablespoons curry powder
- 2 teaspoons salt or to taste
- ½ teaspoon cayenne pepper
- 4 tablespoons lemon or lime juice
- 1 tablespoon coconut oil
- 2 small onions or shallots, minced
- 4 minced tablespoons garlic
- 1 tablespoon coconut sugar
- 2 cans (14 ounces each) coconut milk
- 1 teaspoon turmeric powder

To serve:

- A handful fresh cilantro, chopped, to garnish
- Cooked brown rice

Directions:

1. Select the 'Sauté' button. Add coconut oil and allow it to melt.
2. Add the onion, garlic, ginger, and 2 tablespoons of water and cook until the onion turns translucent.
3. Stir in spices, salt, and coconut sugar.
4. Stir in coconut milk, lentils, and remaining water. Press the 'Cancel' button.
5. Close the lid and lock it by setting the valve to the sealed position. Select the 'Manual' button and set the timer for 15 minutes.
6. When the timer goes off, allow the pressure to release naturally for 10 minutes, after which release the remaining pressure.
7. Stir and garnish with cilantro.
8. Serve over hot cooked brown rice.

QUINOA BURRITO BOWLS

Preparation time: 5 minutes

Cooking time: 20 minutes

Number of servings: 2

Ingredients:

- ½ teaspoon extra-virgin olive oil
- ½ bell pepper, diced
- 1 small red onion, diced
- Salt to taste
- ½ cup quinoa, rinsed
- ½ cup water
- ½ teaspoon ground cumin
- ½ cup salsa
- ¾ cup cooked or canned black beans, drained, rinsed

Optional toppings: Use any

- Red cabbage, shredded
- Lettuce

- Avocado slices
- Onion slices
- Any other toppings of your choice
- Guacamole
- Green onions
- Cilantro
- Salsa
- Lime wedges, etc.

Directions:

1. Select the 'Sauté' button. Add oil. Once the oil is hot enough, add pepper and onion and sauté until slightly tender.
2. Stir in cumin and salt. Press the 'Cancel' button.
3. Add the remaining ingredients and stir.
4. Select the 'Rice' button and set the timer for 20 minutes. When the timer goes off, uncover and loosen the quinoa with a fork.
5. Divide into 2 bowls. Place any of the suggested serving options on top and serve.

MOROCCAN LENTILS

Preparation time: 10 minutes

Cooking time: 15 minutes

Number of servings: 4

Ingredients:

- ½ cup whole brown lentils
- 1 carrot, peeled, chopped
- 1 stalk celery, chopped
- ½ teaspoon salt
- ½ can (from a 19 ounce can) diced tomatoes with its juices
- 2 onions, diced
- 2 cups cubed sweet potatoes
- ½ teaspoon paprika
- ¼ teaspoon ground cinnamon
- 1/8 teaspoon ground cloves
- 1/8 teaspoon ground ginger
- ½ teaspoon garlic powder
- ½ teaspoon ground cumin

- ½ teaspoon onion powder
- 1/8 teaspoon cayenne pepper or more to taste
- 1 cup vegetable stock
- ½ tablespoon maple syrup

To serve:

- A handful parsley, chopped
- ½ tablespoon lemon juice
- Hot cooked brown rice

Directions:

1. Add all the ingredients into the cooking pot in the instant pot and stir.
2. Close the lid and lock it by setting the valve to the sealed position. Select the 'Manual' button and set the timer for 15 minutes.
3. When the timer goes off, allow the pressure to release naturally for 10 minutes, after which release the remaining pressure.
4. Add lemon juice. Stir and garnish with parsley.
5. Serve over hot cooked brown rice.

SPINACH MUSHROOM PASTA

Preparation time: 15 minutes

Cooking time: 15 minutes

Number of servings: 3 – 4

Ingredients:

For pasta:

- 2 cups water
- 6 ounces gluten-free penne pasta or whole wheat penne pasta

Other ingredients:

- 2 tablespoons olive oil
- 3 cloves garlic, minced
- 3 Roma tomatoes, chopped
- 1 cup sliced mushrooms
- 2 cups chopped fresh spinach
- ½ cup chopped onion
- 1 cup cooked white beans

- ½ tablespoon red pepper flakes
- ½ tablespoon sea salt or to taste
- ½ tablespoon Italian seasoning
- 1 tablespoon grated vegan parmesan cheese, to garnish
- 1 sprig fresh basil, to garnish

Directions:

1. Add pasta and water into the cooking pot in the instant pot.
2. Close the lid and lock it by setting the valve to the sealed position. Select the 'Manual' button and set the timer for 4 minutes.
3. When the timer goes off, quickly release all the pressure.
4. Transfer into a strainer and rinse under cold running water. Set aside.
5. Wipe the pot clean.
6. Select the 'Sauté' button. Add oil. Once the oil is hot enough, add the onion, spinach, garlic, mushrooms, beans, and all the spices and mix well. Cook for about 5 – 8 minutes.

7. Stir in tomatoes and cook until the tomatoes are soft. Blend most of the vegetable mixture with an immersion blender until smooth.

8. Stir in pasta.

9. Sprinkle basil and vegan parmesan on top and serve.

LENTIL LOAF

Preparation time: 15 minutes

Cooking time: 60 – 70 minutes

Number of servings: 4 – 5

Ingredients:

- ½ cup chopped onion
- 1 ½ cups water
- ¼ cup uncooked brown rice
- ¼ teaspoon dried thyme
- ¾ – 1 cup finely chopped mushrooms
- ¾ cup dry uncooked lentils, rinsed
- 2 small bay leaves
- ½ tablespoons tahini

Other ingredients:

- 1 tablespoon ground flax seed
- 1 ½ tablespoons walnuts (optional)
- ½ teaspoon garlic powder

- ½ teaspoon ground cumin
- ½ teaspoon dried oregano
- ¼ teaspoon paprika
- 1 – 2 teaspoons soy sauce
- 1/8 cup water
- 1 teaspoons chili powder
- ½ teaspoon onion powder
- 1 tablespoon tomato paste
- ¼ tablespoon vegan Worcestershire sauce

For tomato maple glaze: optional

- 2 tablespoons tomato paste
- ¾ tablespoon apple cider vinegar
- ½ teaspoon paprika
- 1 tablespoon maple syrup
- ½ tablespoon soy sauce

Directions:

1. Select the 'Sauté' button. Add mushrooms and onions and cook for 2 minutes without adding any water or oil.

2. Add 1 ½ cups of water, rice, lentils, bay leaves, tahini, and thyme. Stir until well combined. Press the 'Cancel' button.

3. Close the lid and lock it by setting the valve to the sealed position. Select the 'Manual' button and set the timer for 10 minutes.

4. When the timer goes off, allow the pressure to release naturally. Discard the bay leaves.

5. Combine all the other ingredients in a bowl.

6. Transfer into the instant pot and mix well.

7. Transfer the lentil mixture into a loaf pan.

8. Preheat the oven to 400°F and bake for about 30 minutes or until brown on top.

9. To make tomato maple glaze: Combine all the glaze ingredients in a bowl.

10. Spread this glaze all over the top of the lentil loaf halfway through baking.

11. Remove from the oven and let cool for a few minutes.

12. Slice and serve.

TOFU & GREEN BEANS CURRY

Preparation time: 10 minutes

Cooking time: 15 minutes

Number of servings: 4

Ingredients:

- 14 ounces green beans, trimmed, cut into 1 ½ inch pieces
- 1 ½ cups canned coconut milk
- 2 ½ tablespoons peanut butter
- 2 teaspoons coconut oil
- 6 – 7 teaspoons curry paste
- 1 dried red chili, broken into pieces or add more chili to taste
- 3 tablespoons cashews
- 1 ½ teaspoons grated garlic
- 1 ½ teaspoons grated ginger
- A large pinch turmeric powder
- 2 ½ teaspoons rice vinegar
- 1/3 cup water

- 1 medium onion, chopped
- ½ teaspoon vegan fish sauce
- ¾ coconut sugar
- ¾ teaspoon soy sauce
- 2 ½ teaspoons lemon juice
- 7 ounces extra-firm tofu, drained cut into cubes
- Salt to taste
- Cooked brown rice, to serve

Directions:

1. Place green beans in the cooking pot in the instant pot. Pour a cup of water over them.

2. Close the lid and lock it by setting the valve to the sealed position. Select the 'Manual' button and set the timer for 5 minutes.

3. When the timer goes off, quickly release extra pressure. Drain the green beans and wipe the pot clean. Set them aside.

4. Select the 'Sauté' button. Let the pot heat. Add oil and allow it to heat. Add dried chili and stir for a few seconds.

5. Stir in the onion and cook for a couple of minutes.

6. Next add cashews and stir for a minute. Next add in the turmeric, garlic, and ginger. Cook for a few seconds until aromatic. Select the 'Cancel' button.

7. Combine coconut milk, peanut butter, curry paste, and water in a bowl and pour into the pot. Mix well.

8. Add tofu, rice vinegar, sugar, soy sauce, vegan fish sauce, and salt and mix well.

9. Close the lid and lock it by setting the valve to the sealed position. Select the 'Manual' button and set the timer for 2 minutes.

10. When the timer goes off, release the extra pressure.

11. Select the 'Sauté' button. Add green beans and stir. Simmer for a couple of minutes.

12. Serve hot over hot cooked brown rice.

CHAPTER 12:
MEDITERRANEAN DIET SIDE DISH RECIPES

RATATOUILLE

Preparation time: 15 minutes

Cooking time: 10 minutes

Number of servings: 4

Ingredients:

- ½ pound zucchini, cubed
- 1 large bell pepper of any color, chopped into squares

- 1 medium yellow onion, chopped
- 2 cloves garlic, minced
- Salt to taste
- 1 ½ tablespoons tomato paste
- 2 tablespoons olive oil + extra to serve
- ½ pound eggplant, cubed
- ½ pound tomatoes, chopped
- A handful fresh basil, chopped
- Salt to taste

Directions:

1. Select the 'Sauté' button. Add oil and allow it to heat.
2. Add the onions and a bit of salt and sauté until light brown.
3. Add tomato paste and mix well.
4. Add the rest of the ingredients except salt. Mix well. Sprinkle some water and stir. Press the 'Cancel' button.
5. Close the lid and lock it by setting the valve to the sealed position. Select the 'Manual' button and set the timer for 4 minutes.

6. When the timer goes off, quickly release all the pressure. Add salt and stir.

7. Sprinkle to garnish with basil and serve.

BLACK RICE RISOTTO WITH MUSHROOMS AND CARAMELIZED ONIONS

Preparation time: 10 minutes

Cooking time: 45 minutes

Number of servings: 3

Ingredients:

- ½ cup black rice
- 2 teaspoons olive oil
- ½ teaspoon minced garlic
- 6 button mushrooms, sliced
- Salt to taste
- ¼ cup cashews
- Pepper to taste
- 1 tablespoon miso paste or nutritional yeast (optional)
- 2 ½ cups hot vegetable stock or water
- 1 medium onion, chopped
- 1 medium onion, thinly sliced
- 2 tablespoons white wine (optional)

- ½ teaspoon red pepper flakes
- ½ teaspoon sugar (optional)

Directions:

1. To make cashew cheese: Add cashew and miso into a blender. Add a little water and blend until smooth. Set aside.
2. Select the 'Sauté' button. Add ½ the oil and allow it to heat. Add chopped onion and sauté for a couple of minutes.
3. Stir in salt, pepper, and red pepper flakes. Cook for a few minutes until the onion turns translucent.
4. Stir in garlic and cook for about a minute. Press the 'Cancel' button.
5. Add wine and remove any stuck browned bits by scraping the base of the pot.
6. Add salt, pepper, and stock and stir.
7. Close the lid and lock it by setting the valve to the sealed position. Select the 'Multigrain' button and set the timer for 4 minutes.
8. When the timer goes off, quickly release all the pressure.
9. Uncover and add cashew cheese. Mix well.

10. Cover the pot and let it sit for 5 – 6 minutes.

11. While the risotto is cooking, heat a skillet over low flame. Add the remaining oil and allow it to heat. Add sliced onion and cook until caramelized. Turn off the heat and scatter the onions on top of the risotto.

12. Serve hot.

INSTANT POT TWICE BAKED POTATOES

Preparation time: 10 minutes

Cooking time: 35 minutes

Number of servings: 6

Ingredients:

- 6 potatoes
- ½ cup low fat sour cream
- 1/3 cup bacon crumbles
- 1/3 cup chopped green onions
- 6 tablespoons butter
- 2/3 cup milk
- 1 ½ cups shredded cheddar cheese
- Pepper to taste
- Salt to taste

Directions:

1. Using a fork, prick the potatoes all over. Pour 1 ½ cups water into the cooking pot in the instant pot.

2. Place a trivet in the pot and arrange the potatoes over it.

3. Close the lid and lock it by setting the valve to the sealed position. Select the 'Manual' button and set the timer for 20 minutes if the potatoes are medium size or 25 minutes if the potatoes are large.

4. When the timer goes off, quickly release all the pressure. Discard the water from the pot.

5. Place the potatoes on your cutting board. Once they are cool enough to touch, cut them into 2 halves lengthwise.

6. Using a spoon, scoop out some of the potatoes to make potato cases. Remove as much as possible, but leave a portion of the flesh near the skin.

7. Add the scooped potato into a bowl. Pour in the milk and sour cream. Add butter and mash well using a potato masher.

8. Add a cup of cheddar cheese, salt, and pepper and mix well.

9. Fill this mixture into the potato cases.

10. Pour 1 cup of water into the cooking pot in the instant pot.

11. Place a trivet in the pot and arrange the stuffed potatoes over it.

12. Scatter the remaining cheddar cheese on top. Scatter bacon crumbles over the cheese.

13. Close the lid and lock it by setting the valve to the sealed position. Select the 'Manual' button and set the timer for 5 minutes.

14. When the timer goes off, quickly release all the pressure. Remove the potatoes from the pot and place on a serving platter.

15. Garnish with green onions and serve.

MEDITERRANEAN VEGETABLES

Preparation time: 10 minutes

Cooking time: 8 minutes

Number of servings: 8

Ingredients:

- 4 tablespoons + 4 teaspoons extra-virgin olive oil, divided
- 2 medium yellow onions, cut into ¼ inch thick wedges
- 4 medium zucchinis, cut into 1/8 slices along their length and then cut into 2 halves crosswise
- 2 small red bell peppers, cut into ¼ inch wide strips
- 4 teaspoons balsamic vinegar
- 4 teaspoons Greek seasoning
- ½ teaspoon sugar (optional)
- ½ teaspoon garlic salt

Directions:

1. Select the 'Sauté' button. Add 4 tablespoons of olive oil into the cooking pot in the instant pot and allow it

to heat. Add the onion and cook until it becomes translucent. Press the 'Cancel' button.

2. Add zucchini and bell pepper and stir. Sprinkle ¼ cup water.

3. Select the 'Manual' button and set the timer for 2 minutes.

4. When the timer goes off, quickly release all the pressure.

5. Meanwhile, add 4 teaspoons olive oil, vinegar, Greek seasoning, sugar, and garlic salt into a bowl and whisk it well.

6. Transfer the vegetables into a bowl. Pour the dressing on top. Toss well and serve.

MEDITERRANEAN RICE

Preparation time: 10 minutes

Cooking time: 20 minutes

Number of servings: 4

Ingredients:

- ½ tablespoon avocado oil
- 1 tablespoon olive oil
- 1 small red bell pepper, finely chopped
- ¼ cup finely chopped onion
- ¼ teaspoon dried oregano
- 1 cup brown rice, rinsed
- ½ tablespoon lemon juice
- ½ tablespoon red wine vinegar
- ¼ teaspoon pepper or to taste
- ¼ cup diced kalamata olives, pitted
- 1 cup water or broth
- Zest of ½ lemon, grated
- Salt to taste

- ½ cup finely chopped English cucumber

Directions:

1. Select the 'Sauté' button. Add avocado oil into the cooking pot in the instant pot and allow it to heat. Add the onion and cook until it becomes translucent.

2. Stir in oregano and red bell pepper and cook for a couple of minutes. Press the 'Cancel' button.

3. Add rice and broth and mix well.

4. Select the 'Rice' button and set the timer for 20 minutes.

5. While the rice cooks, add olive oil, lemon zest, salt, lemon juice, red wine vinegar, and pepper into a bowl and whisk it well.

6. When the timer goes off, uncover and pour the dressing into the pot and mix well.

7. Add more salt and pepper to taste if required.

8. Add cucumbers and olives just before serving. Mix well and serve.

INSTANT POT ARTICHOKES

Preparation time: 20 minutes

Cooking time: 10 minutes

Number of servings: 4

Ingredients:

- 2 cups water
- 4 large artichokes, discard stems
- 2 tablespoons olive oil
- Salt to taste
- Coarsely ground pepper to taste

For garlic mustard dip:

- 2 tablespoons Dijon mustard
- 10 tablespoons mayonnaise
- ½ teaspoon cayenne pepper
- 4 cloves garlic, peeled, minced

Directions:

1. Place the trivet in the instant pot. Pour water into it. Place the artichokes on the trivet, the stem side touching the trivet.

2. Close the lid and lock it by setting the valve to the sealed position. Select the 'Steam' button. Set the timer for 10 minutes.

3. Meanwhile, add all the ingredients for garlic mustard dip into a bowl and whisk it well. Cover and set aside so that the flavors blend together.

4. When the timer goes off, allow the pressure to release naturally for 10 minutes. After that release the extra pressure.

5. Take out the artichokes and set aside to cool for a few minutes. When they are cool enough to handle, cut each artichoke into 2 halves. Discard the white and purple parts.

6. Drizzle the oil over the cut half of the artichokes and spread it with a brush so the cut portion of the artichokes are fully coated.

7. Serve artichoke halves with dipping sauce.

HORTA (GREENS) AND POTATOES

Preparation time: 10 minutes

Cooking time: 25 minutes

Number of servings: 3

Ingredients:

- 1 bunch greens of your choice like spinach, kale, mustard greens, etc., discard hard stems and ribs, chopped
- ½ cup water
- Juice of ½ lemon
- 5 cloves garlic, peeled, sliced
- 3 small potatoes or 2 medium potatoes, rinsed, cut into chunks
- ½ cup extra-virgin olive oil
- Pepper to taste
- Lemon slices to serve
- Salt to taste

Directions:

1. Add all the ingredients except lemon slices into the cooking pot in the instant pot and stir.

2. Close the lid and lock it by setting the valve to the sealed position. Select the 'Manual' button and set the timer for 15 minutes.

3. When the timer goes off, allow the pressure to release naturally for 10 minutes, after which release all the remaining pressure.

4. Stir and serve with lemon wedges.

INSTANT POT CABBAGE

Preparation time: 8 minutes

Cooking time: 3 minutes

Number of servings: 2 – 3

Ingredients:

- 1 pound green cabbage, cut into 2 inch pieces
- 1 medium carrot, cut into ¼ inch thick round slices
- 3 tablespoons water or vegetable broth
- Freshly ground pepper to taste
- ½ large yellow onion, cut into thick slices
- 2 tablespoons butter
- Salt to taste
- Red pepper flakes to taste

Directions:

1. Select the 'Sauté' button. Add butter and water. When the butter melts, add the rest of the ingredients and mix well. Press the 'Cancel' button.

2. Close the lid and lock it by setting the valve to the sealed position. Select the 'Manual' button and set the timer for 3 minutes.

3. When the timer goes off, quickly release all the remaining pressure.

4. Stir and serve with some more pepper sprinkled on top.

SCALLOPED POTATOES

Preparation time: 10 minutes

Cooking time: 20 minutes

Number of servings: 4

Ingredients:

- 1 pound Yukon gold or red potatoes, cut into ¼ inch thick round slices
- Salt to taste
- 1 ½ tablespoons light cream
- Pepper to taste
- ½ cup vegetable broth
- 1 cup shredded sharp cheddar cheese, divided
- ¼ teaspoon garlic powder
- 1/8 teaspoon ground nutmeg

Directions:

1. Add potatoes, salt, and broth into the cooking pot in the instant pot.

2. Close the lid and lock it by setting the valve to the sealed position. Select the 'Manual' button and set the timer for 3 minutes.

3. When the timer goes off, quick release all the remaining pressure.

4. Open the lid and gently empty the contents of the pot into a baking dish.

5. Preheat the oven to 375°F.

6. Add ¾ cup cheddar cheese, spices, and cream into the instant pot and stir.

7. Press the 'Sauté' option and simmer until well combined. Press the 'Cancel' button.

8. Spoon the sauce over the potatoes.

9. Transfer the baking dish into the oven and bake for 15 minutes. If desired, after baking, switch the oven to broil and brown the tops.

10. Garnish with remaining cheddar cheese and serve.

INSTANT POT ROASTED BRUSSELS SPROUTS

Preparation time: 5 minutes

Cooking time: 15 minutes

Number of servings: 6

Ingredients:

- 3 tablespoons olive oil
- 1 ½ pounds whole Brussels sprouts
- Pepper to taste

- 2 medium onions, chopped
- Salt to taste
- ¾ cup vegetable broth

Directions:

1. Select the 'Sauté' button. Add oil into the cooking pot in the instant pot and allow it to heat. Add the onions and cook until they become soft.

2. Stir in Brussels sprouts and stir-fry for a couple of minutes. Season with salt and pepper. Press the 'Cancel' button.

3. Drizzle broth over the Brussels sprouts.

4. Close the lid and lock it by setting the valve to the sealed position. Select the 'Manual' button and set the timer for 3 minutes.

5. When the timer goes off, allow the pressure to release naturally for 3 – 4 minutes, after which release all the remaining pressure.

6. Stir well and serve.

CHAPTER 13:
MEDITERRANEAN DIET DESSERT RECIPES

MEDITERRANEAN DIET FRIENDLY CAKE

Preparation time: 15 minutes

Cooking time: 60 minutes

Number of servings: 6 – 7

Ingredients:

- 1 ¼ cups +1 tablespoon whole wheat flour + extra to dust
- 2/3 teaspoon baking powder
- 2/3 teaspoon baking soda
- ¼ teaspoon salt
- 2/3 cup sugar
- 2 eggs
- ½ cup extra-virgin olive oil
- ½ cup whole milk
- 2/3 teaspoon vanilla extract

- ½ teaspoon grated lemon zest

Directions:

1. Mix the flour, baking powder, baking soda, and salt together in a bowl and stir until well incorporated.
2. Add eggs and sugar into another bowl and whisk until the sugar dissolves. You can also measure out the sugar first and then powder it before using.
3. Whisk in the milk, lemon zest, oil, and vanilla extract.
4. Add flour mixture a little at a time and fold gently each time.
5. Grease a springform pan or cake pan that can fit well into the instant pot with some cooking spray. Dust with some flour.
6. Pour batter into the pan. Take 2 sheets of foil and cover the pan tightly.
7. Pour 1 ½ cups water into the instant pot. Place a steamer rack or trivet in the pot.
8. Place the cake pan on the steamer rack.
9. Close the lid and lock it by setting the valve to the sealed position. Select the 'Manual' button and set the timer for 35 minutes.
10. When the timer goes off, allow the pressure to release naturally.

11. Remove pan. Uncover and set aside to cool to room temperature.
12. Slice and serve.

APPLE CRISP

Preparation time: 10 minutes

Cooking time: 8 minutes

Number of servings: 6 – 8

Ingredients:

- 4 apples, peeled, cored, chopped
- ½ teaspoon ground nutmeg
- ½ teaspoon vanilla
- 1 ½ tablespoons maple syrup
- 1 ½ tablespoons butter, melted
- 1 ½ tablespoons water
- 1 teaspoon ground cinnamon
- ½ teaspoon ground ginger (optional)
- ½ cup oats
- 1 ½ tablespoons flour

Directions:

1. Spread apples on the bottom of the instant pot accessory pan or any other heat proof container that can fit well inside the instant pot.

2. Sprinkle nutmeg and cinnamon. Add vanilla and mix well. Stir in maple syrup and water. Spread it evenly.

3. Add oatmeal, butter, and flour into a bowl and mix until crumbly.

4. Sprinkle this mixture on top of the apples.

5. Pour a cup of water into the instant pot.

6. Place a steamer rack or trivet in the pot.

7. Place the cake pan on the steamer rack.

8. Close the lid and lock it by setting the valve to the sealed position. Select the 'Manual' button and set the timer for 8 minutes.

9. When the timer goes off, release the extra pressure.

10. This can be served hot or warm.

FRENCH LEMON CRÈME
(POTS DE CRÈME AU CITRON)

Preparation time: 20 minutes

Cooking time: 20 minutes

Number of servings: 3

Ingredients:

- ½ cup skim milk
- 3 egg yolks
- 1/3 cup coconut sugar or erythritol or stevia to taste
- ½ cup fresh cream
- Zest from ½ lemon

To serve:

- ¼ cup blackberries
- Blackberry syrup

Directions:

1. To make lemon zest: Peel the lemon using a peeler into wide strips. The peel forms the zest. The remaining lemon can be used in another recipe.

2. Add milk, lemon zest, and cream into a heavy bottomed saucepan over medium heat. When the mixture starts to bubble, turn off the heat. Let it cool.

3. Combine yolks and sweetener in a bowl and whisk until the sugar dissolves completely. Pour the cooled milk mixture and whisk until well combined.

4. Divide the mixture equally into 3 ramekins and cover each ramekin with foil.

5. Pour 1 ½ cups water into the instant pot. Place a steamer rack or trivet in the pot.

6. Place the ramekins on the steamer rack.

7. Close the lid and lock it by setting the valve to the sealed position. Select the 'Manual' button and set the timer for 10 minutes.

8. When the timer goes off, allow the pressure to release naturally.

9. Remove ramekins. Uncover and set aside to cool to room temperature.

10. Cover each ramekin with cling wrap. Place in the refrigerator for 4 – 5 hours.

11. Garnish blackberries and drizzle blackberry syrup over them and serve.

RICE PUDDING WITH CRANBERRIES

Preparation time: 10 minutes

Cooking time: 15 minutes

Number of servings: 12

Ingredients:

- ½ cup short grain brown rice, rinsed
- 4 teaspoons vanilla extract or 2 vanilla pods, scrape the seeds
- 5 cups almond milk, unsweetened, or more if required
- 4 tablespoons chopped, toasted almonds

- 2 tablespoons coconut palm sugar or honey or more to taste
- ½ cup dried cranberries
- ¼ teaspoon ground cinnamon

Directions:

1. Add rice, milk, vanilla, and coconut sugar into the instant pot and stir.

2. Close the lid and lock it by setting the valve to the sealed position. Select the 'Manual' button and set the timer for 12 minutes.

3. When the timer goes off, allow the pressure to release naturally.

4. Select the 'Sauté' button. If the milk has been absorbed, add more milk as required. Stir frequently. Press the 'Cancel' button. Transfer into a bowl.

5. While the rice is cooking, soak cranberries in lukewarm water for a while. Drain off the water. Squeeze the cranberries and chop into smaller pieces.

6. Sprinkle cinnamon, almonds, and cranberries on top and serve warm or cold.

BREAD PUDDING

Preparation time: 10 minutes

Cooking time: 35 minutes

Number of servings: 4

Ingredients:

- Sugar or swerve sweetener to taste
- 4 cups chopped old bread (3 – 4 days old challah or brioche bread)
- 1 ½ teaspoons vanilla extract
- A large pinch ground cinnamon
- ¼ cup raisins (optional)
- ½ tablespoon butter
- 1 ½ cups light cream
- 1 cup skim milk
- ¼ teaspoon salt
- 2 large eggs
- 3 egg yolks

Directions:

1. If your bread is not old, then spread it on a baking sheet and bake for a few minutes until dry.
2. Grease the instant pot accessory pan with some oil or butter.
3. Place the bread in a bowl.
4. Whisk together the rest of the ingredients except butter, pour over the bread and stir. Set aside for 15 minutes.
5. Place cubes of butter all over the dish.
6. Pour 1 ½ cups of water into the cooking pot in the instant pot. Place a trivet in the pot.
7. Place the dish over the trivet.
8. Close the lid and lock it by setting the valve to the sealed position. Select the 'Manual' button and set the timer for 35 minutes.
9. When the timer goes off, allow the pressure to release naturally.
10. Remove the dish and let it cool completely.
11. Serve warm or chilled.

MIXED BERRY CRUMBLE

Preparation time: 10 minutes

Cooking time: 8 minutes

Number of servings: 4 – 6

Ingredients:

- 1 ½ cups mixed frozen berries
- ¾ cup rolled oats
- 2 tablespoons honey
- ½ teaspoon ground cinnamon
- ¼ cup nonfat vanilla Greek yogurt
- ½ tablespoon Truvia baking blend
- 2 tablespoons whole wheat flour
- 2 tablespoons melted coconut oil
- ¼ teaspoon salt
- ¼ cup nonfat Greek yogurt

Directions:

1. Spread the berries on the bottom of the instant pot accessory pan.

2. Dust with truvia baking blend.
3. Add oats, honey, flour, coconut oil, salt, and cinnamon into a bowl and mix well.
4. Scatter this mixture over the berries.
5. Cover the pan with foil, tightly.
6. Pour 1 ½ cups water into the cooking pot of the instant pot. Set a trivet in it.
7. Place the pan over the trivet.
8. Close the lid and lock it by setting the valve to the sealed position. Select the 'Manual' button and set the timer for 10 minutes.
9. When the timer goes off, allow the pressure to release naturally.
10. Remove the pan from the instant pot and let it cool for 10 minutes.
11. Drizzle yogurt on top and serve.

CRÈME BRULEE

Preparation time: 5 minutes

Cooking time: 20 minutes

Number of servings: 3

Ingredients:

- 2 egg yolks
- ¾ cup heavy cream
- 1/8 cup maple syrup
- A pinch of fine salt
- ½ teaspoon vanilla extract
- 2 tablespoons very fine sugar, to top

Directions:

1. Add yolks, maple syrup, and salt into a bowl and whisk it well. Add the cream and vanilla and whisk until well blended.
2. Pour this mixture into 3 custard cups or ramekins. Cover the cups with aluminum foil.

3. Place a trivet in the cooking pot in the instant pot. Pour about 1 ½ cups of water into the pot.
4. Place the cups on the trivet.
5. Close the lid and lock it by setting the valve to the sealed position. Select the 'Manual' button and set the timer for 7 minutes.
6. Once the timer goes off, allow the pressure to release naturally.
7. Remove the cups from the pot once cooled enough to touch. Uncover and cool completely.
8. Sprinkle with fine sugar on top. Caramelize with a culinary torch until golden brown on top. Serve right away or chill and serve later.

POACHED PEARS

Preparation time: 10 minutes

Cooking time: 10 minutes

Number of servings: 6

Ingredients:

- 6 ripe, medium sized pears, peeled, cored, let the stem remain
- 2 sticks cinnamon
- 4 cups fresh grape juice or orange juice
- ½ inch piece fresh ginger, peeled, sliced
- 3 tablespoons lemon juice
- 2 star anise
- 1 teaspoon ground cinnamon, to garnish

Directions:

1. Add all the ingredients except ground cinnamon to the cooking pot in the instant pot.

2. Close the lid and lock it by setting the valve to the sealed position. Select the 'Manual' button and timer for 8 minutes.

3. Once the timer goes off, quickly release the excess pressure.

4. Sprinkle the ground cinnamon on top of each pear and serve warm or chilled.

PUMPKIN CUSTARD

Preparation time: 10 minutes

Cooking time: 20 minutes

Number of servings: 12

Ingredients:

- 2 cans (15 ounces each) pumpkin puree
- 1 cup coconut milk
- 2 eggs
- 5 – 6 tablespoons maple syrup or honey or 1 packet stevia
- ¼ teaspoon ground ginger (optional)
- 1 teaspoon pumpkin pie spice
- A pinch salt

Directions:

1. Pour 1 ½ cups of water into the instant pot. Place a trivet in it.
2. Blend together all the ingredients in a blender until well combined. Grease 12 heatproof ramekins or use the instant pot pan insert and pour the blended

mixture into the ramekins or pan. Fill each 2/3 full. Cover the ramekins with foil.

3. Place the ramekins or pan in the pot. You can stack them or cook them in batches if using ramekins.

4. Close the lid and lock it by setting the valve to the sealed position. Select the 'Manual' button and set the timer for 20 minutes.

5. Once the timer goes off, allow the pressure to release naturally.

6. Remove the cups from the pot once cool enough to touch. Uncover and cool completely.

7. Serve right away, or serve warmed or chilled later.

CONCLUSION

On that sugary-sweet note, we have reached the end of the book. It has been a long journey, and I sincerely hope you found the recipes exciting. You must be raring to head to the kitchen and whip up a storm!

The recipes shared with you are all easy to prepare, and the instant pot makes your job even easier by cooking your meals in a jiffy. The ingredients used in these recipes are all locally available, so you don't have to worry about sourcing exotic ingredients. If you follow the recipes properly, your end result will be perfect and you can boast about your cooking skills without sweating long hours in the kitchen.

By now you know that the Mediterranean diet is not just healthy but also extremely tasty, too. More than a dietary change, it is a healthy eating pattern that will help your overall well-being. Cooking your food in an Instant Pot ensures that your food is cooked well and fast, and you don't have to spend hours in the kitchen to cook your meals.

So what are you waiting for? Pick the recipe you like best and get started. Thank you once again for choosing this book, and

I hope you enjoyed the recipes. Happy cooking and good luck!

Leave the review

As an independent author with a small marketing budget, reviews are my livelihood on this platform. If you enjoyed this book, I'd really appreciate it if you left your honest feedback.

REFERENCES

Mediterranean diet: A heart-healthy eating plan. (2019). Mayo Clinic website: https://www.mayoclinic.org/healthy-lifestyle/nutrition-and-healthy-eating/in-depth/mediterranean-diet/art-20047801

Martini D. (2019). Health Benefits of Mediterranean Diet. *Nutrients*, *11*(8), 1802. https://doi.org/10.3390/nu11081802

Scarmeas, N., Stern, Y., Tang, M. X., Mayeux, R., & Luchsinger, J. A. (2006). Mediterranean diet and risk for Alzheimer's disease. *Annals of neurology*, *59*(6), 912–921. https://doi.org/10.1002/ana.20854

Printed in Great Britain
by Amazon